Routledge
New York and London

PUBERTY, SEXUALITY, AND THE SELF

Boys and Girls at Adolescence

Karin A. Martin

Published in 1996
by Routledge
29 West 35th Street
New York, NY 10001

Published in
Great Britain by
Routledge
11 New Fetter Lane
London EC4P 4EE

Copyright © 1996 by
Routledge
Printed in the
United States of America
on acid-free paper.

Library of Congress Cataloging-in-Publication-Data

Martin, Karin A.
 Puberty, sexuality, and the self: girls and boys at adolescence/
Karin A. Martin.
  p. cm.
 Includes bibliographical references.
 ISBN 0415-91424-8 (hb).—ISBN 0-415-91425-6 (pb)
  1. Teenagers—United States—Sexual behavior. 2. Puberty—United
States. 3. Adolescence—United States. 4. Adolescent psychology—
United States. I. Title.
HQ27.M37 1996
305.23'5—dc20   96-25060
                                 CIP

PUBERTY, SEXUALITY, AND THE SELF

DEDICATION

To
Christine Ann Martin
and
Jon Herbert Martin

ACKNOWLEDGMENTS

ACKNOWLEDGMENTS FIRST must go to the teenagers who participated in the interviews collected here. They talked with great openness about their personal lives and were eager to help by lending their voices to this project. Similarly, many thanks to the superintendents, principals, and teachers who allowed me into their schools and helped me overcome many of the barriers to interviewing about a difficult topic like sex. Unfortunately, they must remain nameless in order to protect the anonymity of their schools and students.

Many people have helped me to shape the ideas and research in this book. Nancy Chodorow provided me with six years of mentoring and training in feminist theory and psychoanalysis that culminated in this book. Her advice, intellect, and criticisms have been invaluable. I am also grateful to Margaret

Cerullo and Maureen Mahoney for teaching me to think critically about adolescence, sexuality, and psychoanalysis.

Bob Blauner, Christina Maslach, Jane Fargnoli, Anne Sanow, and Barrie Thorne all made comments on earlier drafts of this manuscript that significantly contributed to my thinking and revisions. I am especially grateful to Barrie Thorne for a thoughtful, detailed reading of the manuscript that was critical in the final shaping of it.

I could not have completed this project without the friendship and help of Elizabeth Armstrong and Arona Ragins. Elizabeth Armstrong and I have mixed personal and academic friendship from the moment we began graduate school together. For years, we have been engaged in one long conversation about feminism, sexuality, sociology, and personal life that has deeply influenced my thinking. Her comments and advice on countless drafts of chapters have been critical to the final project. Similarly, Arona Ragins has provided me with both colleaugeship and friendship. Her criticisms of many drafts and our long discussions about teenagers have been invaluable, as has her listening, commiserating, and cheering me up when I needed it.

I also owe many thanks to my family. My brother, Jon Martin, and I had many enlightening conversations about teenage boys, and he shared the trials and tribulations of an academic project with me. I am especially grateful to my parents, Jack and Chris Martin, for encouraging me, supporting my decisions, and generally having faith in me. Finally, I could not have completed this project without the warmth, humor, intelligence, and generosity of Laurie Morgan. She made home a fun and easy place to work and play, and our endless hours of conversation about this project have shaped it immeasurably.

CONTENTS

CONTENTS

x

ADOLESCENT BODIES AND SEXUALITY

Young women are engaged with questions of "being female"; that is, who will control, and to what extent can they control, their own bodies?
—Michelle Fine, *Disruptive Voices*

chapter 1

IN THE course of researching this book, as I sat with one teenage girl after another asking them to tell me about themselves, I heard over and over again lukewarm and critical self-descriptions. Some girls said they were too quiet, while others said they were too loud. Others said they were unhappy with recent decisions they had made. Some girls said they were too sensitive to others' criticisms. Many girls criticized their appearances, and many girls found it difficult to describe themselves at all. Although each girl was different, some shy, some giggly, some poised, some outgoing, most shared this self-critical eye. Boys, in general, did not. Why, I wondered, do adolescent girls think so poorly of themselves?

Research documents a large drop in girls' self-esteem[1] that occurs at adolescence. Therefore, in answering the question of why girls think so poorly of themselves, I looked to adolescence and the experiences that are most transformative at adolescence—puberty and first sex—for an explanation.

Much to the disappointment of many adult women whom I spoke to about my project, I found that in the 1990s gender still profoundly shapes adolescent experiences of sexuality. For example, girls still feel shame about their adult bodies, particularly breast development and menstruation. Girls still "do it" to keep their boyfriends, and boys often "do it" so that they can "go tell their friends, 'Yeah! Yeah!'"

Certainly some things are different about teenage sexuality today compared to forty, or even ten years ago. As Lillian Rubin suggests in her book on the sexual revolution, teenagers today now feel "entitled" to sex.[2] Girls and boys both talk more openly than their parents did about both puberty and sex, and many school systems now provide some form of sex education. Thus, far fewer girls begin menstruating with the fear that they are bleeding to death (although this phenomenon has not disappeared entirely). Masturbation is less taboo for boys and at least sometimes acknowledged for girls. Norms about sexuality are also slightly more accepting. Girls no longer automatically become "sluts" because they have sex. Rather, their age, their reasons for having sex, and the context in which they have sex are judged before labeling them sluts (an admittedly small improvement). There is still, however, no parallel to a slut for boys, although girls do call some boys "himbos," a clever parallel to bimbos.

Despite these changes, many old taboos, feelings of shame, guilt and fear, and gender differentiated experiences still exist and come to the forefront of adolescent life. These gendered experiences of puberty and sex affect adolescents' self-worth. For girls, these experiences lead them to feel badly about themselves, and although it is not "easy" for boys to navigate puberty and first sex either, their selves emerge more intact. These differences are not due to different psychological or biological makeups of girls and boys, but to the gendered cultural meanings that girls and boys learn, absorb, and use to make sense of the world during puberty and their first sexual experiences.

In the following chapter I examine these ideas about body, sexuality and self further. Chapter Three examines in detail how puberty—menarche, breasts development, masturbation, voice change, shaving, weight gain—affects boys' and girls' selves differently. Chapter Four examines teenagers romantic and sexual relationships, particularly girls' propensity for "ideal love." It discusses the different expectations girls and boys have of sex, how they make decisions to have sex with each other, and how they differently experience first sex. In Chapter Five I look at parents' influences on adolescents selves, agency, and sexual subjectivity. Chapter Six and Chapter Seven ask where the possibilities are—school, sports, feminism, mothers—for girls to construct a positive sense of self and sexual subjectivity. It also asks what social changes might help facilitate more agency and sexual subjectivity in adolescent girls and eventually adult women. Before continuing, however, let me describe what interviewing teenagers about puberty, sex, and self is like.

"IT'S JUST LIKE WHAT THE DOCTOR ASKS YOU": INTERVIEWING ADOLESCENTS

Because most research on puberty and teenage sexuality has not examined in detail *how* adolescents subjectively experience changes in their bodies and their sexuality or how these changes affect their senses of self, I conducted a qualitative study, consisting of fifty-five semi-structured, in-depth interviews with adolescent girls and boys from the ages of fourteen to nineteen. (See Methodological Appendix and Interview Schedule for more detail.) The relationships between puberty, sexuality, and sense of self are clearly present in the interviewees' narratives.

In choosing interviewing as my method, I assumed that the best way to find out how people feel about themselves and what makes them feel that way is to ask them. Of course people can lie in interviews, just as they can on surveys. However, it is more difficult to lie or tell half-truths in open-ended interviews, because the inconsistencies in a story become visible. Some of the most interesting data I gathered is found in these inconsistencies which reveal the interviewees struggling with an issue. When I turned off the tape recorder at the end of the interview, I would sometimes hear "the rest of the story." Also, the interviewees told me *stories*, versions of "true" experience, told retrospectively, and constructed partially by the interview setting, myself, and the questions I asked.[3] But the fact that these stories were constructed in this setting does not mean that they are not at the same time versions of or pieces of actual social experiences that we can study.

Researchers always face a set of problems when setting out on a project, and I faced several. First, since people reconstruct experience in light of their present lives, the best way to have done this study would have been longitudinally. Since most interviewees had completed puberty by the time of the interview, this presented a problem with regard to questions about pubertal experience. However, given a lack of resources for such a time-consuming and expensive study, interviewing teens who had just recently reached puberty was a reasonable compromise. In fact, interviewing older adolescents had some advantages. In a face-to-face interview, teens who are just beyond puberty may be better able to articulate what happened to them than those who are in the throes of puberty and who are either uncomfortable with or unsure about what is happening to them. Teens are also still close enough to puberty not to have distorted their experiences much, and many had recently had sex for the first time or were thinking of "doing it" soon. Finally, if one were to longitudinally study pubertal experience, she would run the risk of distorting the experience for the adolescent and therefore distorting her data.

Puberty and sex are difficult topics to discuss, especially for adolescents.[4] I was concerned about how much adolescents would be willing to say to me, and even if they would agree to be interviewed, given the formidable consent form they were presented. As it turned out, they were more willing than I expected. Most of the girls and the middle-class boys seemed to enjoy telling me their stories. Girls were more forthcoming than boys, and middle-class adolescents were more talkative than working-class ones. This class difference seems to result from school structure. There was an insistent authority and lack of freedom in the working-class school where I interviewed, especially compared to the open campus, almost college-like atmosphere of the private schools. Students were constantly being told to "Get to class," or asked "Where are you supposed to be?" or "Do you have a pass?" or told, "You're late. Go to the office." Working-class adolescents, in the more authoritative school structure, were not used to adults asking them to discuss their feelings and opinions at length and often stayed within the boundaries of the interview structure more than middle-class adolescents did.

Interviewing teenage girls was easier than interviewing teenage boys. Since I am a woman, the teenage girls tended to treat me as something between a sex education teacher and an older friend. Several girls made comments throughout the interview like "I've just got to tell you this!" Interviewing adolescent boys about sex was more difficult.[5] Boys are reluctant to volunteer for such interviews and often reluctant to speak. Sharon Thompson writes that during her project she repeatedly had to raise the age of her male interview subjects, and finally she abandoned interviewing boys entirely.

> By the end of the project I was reduced to interviewing twenty-five-year-old boys, who told me in tones suggesting that they were baring their chests for the good of the project, pubertal anecdotes revolving mainly around early heterosexual play or disconnected homosexual episodes like circle jerks.[6]

I did not fare quite so badly. It *was* more difficult to persuade boys to volunteer to be interviewed. Most teachers and principals knew that it would be difficult to convince boys to participate and chalked it up to the character of adolescent boys. I originally wanted to remedy this problem of depending on good-hearted, interested volunteers by paying interviewees ten dollars each for the interview and hoping this would motivate more reluctant students. However, the principals of the schools thought this inappropriate. I began asking the boys and girls whom I did interview why they thought I was having a more difficult time enticing the boys. As they put it,

It's probably sensitivity. Boys tend not to, they don't really want to get sensitive or anything. I think boys are a lot more lazy myself. I'm a class officer and whenever we do anything we always have about twice as many girls as boys. Almost everything [activity] I'm in at school has more girls.

—Marc

Umm, they don't want to do it. They're too chicken. I don't know. "It's stupid. It's queer. What's my benefit out of this?" We're just kind of lazy.

—Paul

However, those who did volunteer were generally willing to talk, although they were not as articulate as girls when it came to discussions of relationships[7] and their actual experiences of sex. Boys were less reflective about their experiences and seemed to have thought less about these issues than girls. The younger age of the male interviewees and the fact that they tended to be boys who were responsible and involved in school (in student council or other school organizations) may account for these differences. Although this group may not be representative of all the boys in these schools, this possibly biased sample probably leads me to *underestimate* gender differences at adolescence. The boys that my study is missing are the stereotypic braggers, those boys whose experiences would be even more different from girls. Furthermore, childhood ethnographer Barrie Thorne has noted that the type of boys who *are* in my sample are understudied. She suggests that quiet, good, well-behaved boys who are not aggressively masculine often get lost in studies of children.[8]

As a female interviewer, boys responded differently to me than they would have to a male interviewer. This is especially true given that I was talking to them about puberty and sex. I do not think what they told me was untrue, but perhaps it was only one version of the story that boys tell. Boys are, however, familiar with talking seriously to women about sexuality.[9] Mothers tend to be the ones who teach boys about sex when they are young. All but one of the male interviewees said their mothers were involved in teaching them about puberty and sex. Often mothers were the only one who talked to them about it. Also, most sex education teachers are women, and this was true at the schools where I interviewed.

Boys seemed to put me in the role of a sex education teacher or doctor,[10] and told me more of the "facts" of pubertal and sexual events and less of the story of the events than girls did. At the end of the interview I asked interviewees what they thought of it, and most of the boys (and girls) said that it was not as embarrassing as they thought it was going to be, given the consent form they had to sign. No one said it was embarrassing, and no one refused to answer any particular question.

5

Boys' discussions about sex with fathers and other men are quite different from those with women. We know that fathers and men tend to gender type children more than mothers and women do.[11] My data shows that when fathers do talk to boys about sex, it is often in the vein of joking or boasting about sex and women or warning them to use condoms. Thus, a male interviewer might elicit more of the boastful, exaggerated stories that boys are often said to tell about sex. Although I think a male interviewer might elicit *different* material from teenage boys, I am not convinced that he would gather more *truthful* stories about puberty and sex.[12]

Boys, however, were not the most reluctant subjects I interviewed. Two Asian-American teens—a boy and a girl—whose families were recent immigrants, had little to say about puberty and sexuality. (Two other Asian-American adolescents whose families were not such recent immigrants were no different in their amount of talk than other teens.) Chan suggests that it would be very difficult to interview such teens about the topics in this study. She explains,

> The distinction between the public and private selves is an important concept in most Asian cultures. The public self is that which conforms to gendered and familial role expectations, behaves in a manner in accordance with social norms, and seeks to avoid actions that would bring shame not only upon oneself but also upon one's family. Sexuality would rarely be expressed in the context of one's public self. Only within the context of the private self can such a subject find easy expression. The private self is never seen by anyone other than one's most intimate family and friends (in some cases, a person may choose never to reveal a private self to anyone).[13]

Chan cautions us that we should not confuse the reluctance to talk about sex with asexuality.

In the next chapter, I examine the stories that other theorists tell us or fail to tell us about gender, sexuality, and the self. I ask how those stories can be modified to help us understand the voices of the teens we hear throughout the following chapters.

THEORIZING SEXUAL SUBJECTIVITY, GENDER, AND ADOLESCENCE

But the only hunger I have ever known was the hunger for sex and the hunger for freedom and somehow, in my mind and heart, they were related and certainly not mutually exclusive.

> —Cherrie Moraga, *Loving in the War Years*

chapter 2

MANY RESEARCHERS have been trying to answer the question of why adolescent girls think so poorly of themselves, but none have looked closely at puberty or first experiences of sex.[14] In particular, the American Association of University Women's study of adolescent self-esteem and the work of Carol Gilligan and her colleagues have received much popular and academic attention.[15] The main finding of these studies is that, although boys' self-esteem drops somewhat at adolescence, girls' sense of self dwindles and their self-esteem drops significantly more than boys' does.[16] Girls, these studies find, silence what they know, are unhappy with themselves, and become less interested in school, especially in math and science.

Brown and Gilligan's new work on adolescent girls is the most theoretically developed piece of all this new research. Their new work follows "women's psychological development back through girls' adolescence and then further back into girls' childhood…"[17] At adolescence, Gilligan and her colleagues "witness a relational crisis in women's psychology."[18] This crisis is a "relational impasse" in which girls give up "authentic" relationship for the sake of maintaining any relationship. Girls lose what Brown and Gilligan call their "authentic selves," the selves of childhood. Girls then find themselves in relationships that are not "real" or "genuine." Brown and Gilligan's definition of a genuine relationship is one in which a girl "can say what she thinks is right, in which conflict and disagreement and strong feelings can occur."[19] They claim that at adolescence girls "lose" these relationships, and become disconnected and dissociated from others and from themselves. They silence themselves.[20]

The authors assume that "genuine" relationships are *always* better, more desirable, and less psychologically damaging than "inauthentic" relationships. However, inauthentic relationships can be instrumental and less damaging than authentic ones in social contexts where there is unequal power. They are useful for people who are in a variety of subordinate positions on a day-to-day basis. Brown and Gilligan, however, ignore power inequities in the social lives of the girls they study.

Brown and Gilligan and other of Gilligan's colleagues see childhood as the time in a girl's life when she is her most authentic self. They romanticize childhood as a time when girls speak their minds, are not oppressed, and are strong and proud. From statistics on abuse, sexual abuse, and inequalities in schooling, we know that childhood is not an entirely carefree time for most girls. I view this romanticization of childhood as a kind of psychological essentialism. Essentialist/cultural feminism imagines cultures and historical moments where strong, unoppressed women ruled in the past. Essentialist gay theorists search for evidence of past cultures where gay people were not oppressed. Somehow unearthing these (real or imaginary) cultures provides communities with an almost utopian vision for which to strive. Gilligan and colleagues do this psychologically. In their model women's authentic selves are the selves they possess before age eleven. This is highly problematic and infantilizing. Are adult women supposed to reclaim the "real" selves they had at age eight?

Also, according to Brown and Gilligan, girls' development is "marked by a series of disconnections and dissociations," in other words the loss of "genuine" relationships. This is not a new way of thinking about adolescence. Understanding adolescence as a time of disconnection and separation is a longstanding tradition represented by theorists like Erikson.[21] Gilligan herself has critiqued those who understand development as moving from connection to separation,[22] and yet she seems to repeat that dominant view in her work on adolescent girls.

There is, however, a larger problem with Brown and Gilligan's theory about why girls loose self-esteem, and this problem is repeated in other new research on girls' self-esteem. This new research explains the change in girls' sense of self by pointing to failures in schools and failures in girls' mentors, especially teachers, mothers, and other adult women. For instance, Brown and Gilligan suggest that teachers and mothers teach girls to be "nice and kind" and to "silence" what they really feel.

Like Brown and Gilligan, the AAUW[23] and the Sadkers[24] trace the problem to schools and teachers who treat girls differently from boys. However, these are not convincing explanations for the change in adolescent girls' feelings about themselves. These explanations cannot tell us why the negative change in girls' selves occurs *at this time*, at adolescence. Why when girls reach age eleven or twelve does their self-worth suddenly begin to drop? Girls are in school and have mothers and teachers telling them to be nice and polite, and treating them differently from boys throughout childhood. Why does it suddenly diminish their self-esteem at adolescence?

The glaring omission in this research is its failure to consider the effects of puberty and first sex, especially differential effects of puberty and sexuality for boys and girls.[25] Puberty is the new event that happens at age eleven or twelve for girls and is loaded with cultural meanings about gender and sexuality. As Laumann et al.'s comprehensive survey on sex in the United States suggests, "Sexual well-being and overall well-being are intricately connected."[26] This book argues that differential experiences of puberty, along with first sexual experiences, given that first sex follows closely on the heels of puberty for many teens, lead girls to feel more negatively about themselves than it does boys.

There is some evidence to suggest that puberty is a more stressful event for girls than boys.[27] Social psychologists, Simmons and Blyth, find that puberty is more stressful for girls and may lower their self-esteem because it corresponds with the transition to junior high school. However, their research does not ask if the experience of puberty itself might carry with it gendered meanings.

In general, little research has been done on how body and sexuality become parts of a gendered self. In their pursuit of women's freedom, many feminists focus their efforts on achieving economic and political equality. They argue that women's freedom will be achieved with equal access to economic resources and to the political sphere. Others focus their efforts on eliminating sexual violence—rape, incest, harassment, and assault. While all these endeavors are absolutely necessary, feminists often overlook the everyday, internal dimensions of women's oppression. Bettina Aptheker argues that women's oppression

> ...involves an internal corrosion, a loss of esteem, a loss of confidence in
> one's knowledge, an inability to give expression to experience. To under-

> stand the colonization of women is to understand its interior dimensions, its psychological consequences, its hold on the imagination, and the enormity of effort, collective and individual, which is required to break its cycle.[28]

This book argues that this "internal corrosion" often includes an alienation from one's bodily and sexual self. This alienation is particularly lethal because it is in large part from our bodies and sexuality that we derive agency and subjectivity throughout our lives. By *sexuality* I mean the pleasure we get from our bodies and the experience of living in a body. I do not mean exclusively genital sexuality, although I include genital sexuality as an important component. I do not propose or assume the content of sexuality and desire here. That is, sexuality and sexual agency is important to everyone's construction of self, regardless of whether they construct their sexual identity as heterosexual, bisexual, gay, lesbian or queer, and regardless of what sexual practices they desire. Who one desires to have sex with or which sexual practices one desires are not as important for my purposes here as the issue of whether or not one desires at all.

In particular, sexuality or what I call sexual subjectivity is an important component of agency, feeling like one can do and act. This feeling (agency) is necessary for a positive sense of self. If one feels helpless, unable to act, as if he or she has no ability to affect his or her life, then one will feel poorly about his or her self. Sexual subjectivity is a necessary component of agency and thus of self-esteem. That is, one's sexuality affects her/his ability to act in the world, and to feel like she/he can "will things and make them happen."[29] One must experience a link between agency and body/sexuality.

As infants we all experience this link as we begin to construct a self through our experiences of our bodies and its pleasures. Our first experiences in the world are bodily, and our psychological birth emerges out of the interaction of our physical sensations with our mental processes as infants.[30] Psychological growth arises from a context of emotional and mental interaction as well as bodily experience. Infants perceive their first experiences and learn about the world through the proximity senses—taste, touch, and smell (as opposed to distance senses of sight and hearing).[31] Bodily sensation provides the means for the infant's discovery of the world and the subjects and objects within it. Throughout infancy and into very early childhood, our intense wishes, wants, and wills are experienced in and expressed through the body. Thumb-sucking or sucking on other objects in order to investigate them, using one's hands, exploring one's body, exploring mother's body, molding one's body with mother's body, jumping or running, and expressing what one likes and does not like to do, or eat, or play, are all bodily experiences that children take pleasure in *and* through which they express their own agency and will.

In adolescence the link between agency and body becomes connected to adult genital sexuality. As this link (or lack of it) is established, girls and boys develop differing amounts of sexual subjectivity and therefore different levels of self-esteem. Adolescence is an important time for the establishment of sexual subjectivity and agency because children are trying to construct adult selves at the same time that they are experiencing dramatic changes in their bodies. Throughout this book, I will document a relationship between sexual subjectivity and agency at adolescence and will document gender and class differences in this relationship. I will show that beyond early childhood, adolescence is the moment when the foundations for agency and sexual subjectivity are solidified. As in early childhood, parents are important to development. Adolescents want both to move away from their parents and into the world, and yet they want to remain close enough that someone will be there to recognize their acts of independence, their accomplishments in the world, and their desires (both sexual and not).[32] Although, the role of parents is important to development of self, agency and sexual subjectivity as it is in early childhood, adolescence is not merely a repetition of early childhood as psychoanalysts often characterize it.[33]

Adolescence is also a "more" socially constructed moment of development, and the issues of adolescence are historically specific.[34] Apter suggests that whereas adolescence and puberty were once seen as occurring simultaneously, puberty now is viewed as proceeding adolescence.[35] Thus, adolescence is more socially and less developmentally constructed than early childhood.

Two other things happen at adolescence that make it different from early childhood. One is puberty and the other sex. Puberty is the most rapid period of human growth outside of neonatal growth and adolescents struggle to integrate these new bodies into their selves. Also, many children become "sexually active"—have sexual intercourse—as adolescents. First experiences of sex, at this age, when teens are psychologically trying to construct new selves and coping with a new body, have profound effects on feelings of agency and sexual subjectivity. According to some psychoanalysts, adolescence is the time when sexual selves solidify.[36]

Adolescence is different from early childhood in other ways as well. Whereas early childhood produces more psychopathology in boys, adolescence is considered more difficult for girls and produces more psychopathology in girls.[37] In teaching a course on the sociology of adolescence, I also found that girls experience adolescence as more difficult than boys do as reflected in the titles of my students' papers. Girls titled their papers "Adolescence: The Tumultuous Years," "The Roller Coaster Ride," "A Troubled Adolescence," "The Trials and Tribulations of a Teen Going Through Adolescence" whereas boys' papers were titled, "The Best Years of My Life," "A Seminal Period of My Adolescence," or "Adolescent Fun."

11

This gender difference can be partially attributed to gender norms becoming more rigid at adolescence. Certainly all of childhood is gendered, and young children are expected to act "appropriately" according to their sex/gender. I argue here only that gendered norms are tightened at adolescence. Less range is allowed in activity, appearance, and demeanor. The emergence of femininity, masculinity, and heterosexuality at adolescence is seen as natural. Teenagers are expected to act masculine and feminine and to participate in heterosexual dating. Cultural norms about beauty, weight, appearance, and demeanor become more rigid. In particular, gender norms become more salient, for girls. From early childhood, boys are taunted with "sissy" for behavior considered effeminate. However, tomboys are tolerated and even enjoyed, as children. But at adolescence tomboys are expected to naturally transform into feminine beauties. Otherwise, they risk being labeled lesbians. The expectations that girls will become appropriately feminine and boys appropriately masculine at adolescence also affect boys and girls differently because the gender norms for women are more unattainable, more enforced, and more oppressive than those for men.[38]

The effects of more rigid gender norms, relations with parents, experiences of puberty, and experiences of sex all overlap and build on each other and shape adolescent selves. For example, at adolescence, the identifications and relationships formed with parents in early childhood remain. However, these identifications and relationships and the processes of recognition are complicated by children's changing bodies. Puberty and the tremendous growth spurt that accompanies it create different opportunities for recognition in adolescent boys and girls. Thus, this is a story of how girls have a more difficult time maintaining feelings of self-worth upon the emergence of their new bodies and adult female sexuality.

In our culture it is generally more difficult for women to derive power, positive feelings of self, or agency from adult sexuality. As African-American poet and feminist theorist Audre Lorde puts it:

> In order to perpetuate itself, every oppression must corrupt or distort those various sources of power within the culture of the oppressed that can provide energy for change. For women, this has meant a suppression of the erotic as a considered source of power and information within our lives.[39]

In our society, as Lorde indicates, women are less sexually subjective than men. First, most women, rather than taking pleasure in their bodies, claim to dislike them. Women, unlike men, often admit to not knowing when they are sexually excited or when they want to have sex. In Laumann et al.'s large survey of sexual practices more than one in ten women reported lack of interest

12

in sex, inability to achieve orgasm, finding sex not pleasurable, having difficulty lubricating, experiencing pain during intercourse, and anxiety about performance in the past year.[40] Similarly Sholty et al. finds that 65% of women who *do* orgasm are not happy with the type of orgasms they have.[41] Thus, it is not surprising that columnist Ann Landers' (nonscientific) survey found that 72% of women readers said "hugs and cuddles" were adequate or preferable forms of sexual expression.

These observations are just some of the evidence of the problem psychoanalytic feminist Jessica Benjamin investigates when she asks, "Do women have a desire of their own?"[42] For women, sexual subjectivity is not easily sustained or developed beyond infancy and early childhood. Women often come to feel, consciously or unconsciously, as if they are not agents, not sexual subjects. Benjamin offers a developmental account of how sexual subjectivity and agency become problematic for women. She anchors her explanation in early childhood.[43] However, she exaggerates women's loss of sexual subjectivity, failing to acknowledge or explain that women can construct some sexual subjectivity in some contexts. Also, like most psychoanalytic theory, Benjamin's theory does not look for the foreclosure of sexual subjectivity and agency beyond early childhood. In her model, all (or most all) development is "done" well before adolescence.[44] However, adolescence is a key moment in the diminishing of women's sexual subjectivity, agency, and self-esteem.

Work by sociologists on sexuality corrects some of the problems of a psychoanalytic framework.[45] In particular, it allows us to integrate the cultural, social, and environmental with the psychological more than Blos and other theorists who are focused on only the mother–child relationship. Simon and Gagnon provide descriptions of three levels of "scripting" that help us to understand the sexual and bodily experiences of adolescent boys and girls. They argue that "for behavior to occur something resembling scripting must occur on three distinct levels: cultural scenarios, interpersonal scripts, and intrapsychic scripts."[46] Cultural scenarios, according to Simon and Gagnon, are "the instructional guides that exist at the level of collective."[47] They are the broad cultural guidelines to social life and behavior. However, they alone are too broad and too abstract to fit every situation. Therefore, social actors must improvise in social interaction. Thus, they create interpersonal scripts, where they become "partial scriptwriters" and make cultural scenarios fit the specific context of their interactions. Finally, actors engage in intrapsychic scripting. Intrapsychic scripting is "the symbolic reorganization of reality in ways that make it complicit in realizing more fully the actor's many-layered and sometimes multi-voiced wishes."[48] Thus, throughout this book we will see that girls' lower self-esteem at adolescence and frequent (though not permanent or universal) lack of agency is a product of cultural discourses (i.e. about female sexuality, female bodies, and gender relations), social interactions (with parents

13

and peers), in particular, recognition, and girls' internalizations of each of these.

THE BOYS' STORY.

Psychoanalytic theory suggests that boys begin to become agents and sexual subjects in early childhood. Early childhood may establish the potential for agency and sexual subjectivity in boys, but I will document that at adolescence many boys fulfill this potential. In particular, as they develop through puberty and then first sexual experiences, boys come to solidify feelings of agency and sexual subjectivity.

First, puberty makes boys look older and more adult. Because of this more adult appearance, boys receive more independence and autonomy from parents and more recognition of their actions and accomplishments. With this recognition boys themselves begin to feel older, more grown-up, independent and agentic. Second, changes in boys' bodies at puberty extend their sense of agency and sexual subjectivity. Although some boys feel uncertain about their changing bodies, many take control of these new bodies and use them to feel older. They take pleasure in their new bodies and abilities. For instance, they "play with" their changing voices and make others laugh or pretend to be their fathers on the telephone. This taking pleasure in and controlling of their pubertal bodies is the beginning of a sense of sexual subjectivity for boys. Boys express a sense of a self that *acts in* their bodies. Third, in many ways, puberty allows boys to identify with their fathers and to feel agentic through this identification.

Thus, boys bring to their first sexual experiences selves that are agentic and that have the beginnings of sexual subjectivity. Therefore, when dating a teenage girl, boys have the ability to ask for and (insist on) sex when they want it, and they often do want sex because it reinforces their masculine and adult status. Most of the boys in my sample expected sex to be good, and it was an event to which they looked forward. They had little problem deciding that they wanted to have sex, and usually encouraged (or pressured, depending on whose perspective one takes) their girlfriends to have sex. When their girlfriends consented (or gave in) this made them feel accomplished, as did the actual experience of having sex. After sex, boys feel more agentic, masculine, adult, and bonded with other men. In particular, they feel like they are able to will something and make it happen, and to do so in the realm of sexuality. Connell reports from his collection of life histories with men that a thirty-year-old man told him that after having sex at age fourteen he felt like a whole new person. "And then during that week I had a whole new sense of myself. I expected—I don't know what I expected, to start growing more pubic hair, or expected my dick to get bigger. But it was that sort of week, you know.

Then after that I was on my way."[49] Thus, first sexual experiences further extend boys' feelings of sexual subjectivity.

THE GIRLS' STORY.

In early childhood girls establish a propensity for ideal love (a way of vicariously achieving agency and sexual subjectivity) and their potential for establishing agency and sexual subjectivity is diminished.[50] However, I will document that as girls develop through adolescence this potential is more thoroughly foreclosed.

As girls reach puberty and enter the new realm of adult female sexuality, they feel ambivalent about growing up and anxious about their new bodies. Because female sexuality in our culture is associated with dirt, shame, taboo, and danger, girls are scared and unsure of their new bodies. Girls' bodies also become objectified by others who perceive them as more sexual as they go through puberty and begin to look older. These pubertal experiences cause girls to dislike their bodies, objectify their own bodies, and act on (rather than in) their own bodies. They rarely take pleasure in and often feel that they are not in control of their bodies. Thus, girls emerge from puberty feeling less agentic and less sexually subjective.

Girls then bring these selves that are constructed at puberty to their first sexual experiences. For girls, first sexual experiences often arise in the context of ideal love. Although girls have negative expectations of sex, they have sex because they fear losing their boyfriends (their ideal love and vicarious agency) if they do not. Few girls actively decide to have sex. For many, sex "just happens," or they "give in" to pressure from boys. After sex, girls are usually unsure of their decisions. Often they do not know if sex was something they wanted, willed and made happen or not. Also, first sex often physically hurts because girls are not sexually excited, and so it allows girls little chance to take pleasure in their bodies. Thus, first experiences of sex, often make girls feel less agentic, less sexually subjective. Girls then emerge from adolescence with what other researchers have called low self-esteem.[51]

CLASS AND OTHER SOCIO–CULTURAL DIFFERENCES.

Class, race, ethnicity, and sexual preference all add exceptions, depth, and specificity to the gendered stories presented above. In this book, I examine these differences in my data and draw on previous research where my data are limited.

The primary axis of difference that I discuss is class. First, middle-class teens were more articulate about their selves in general than working-class teens. This may be attributed to the greater focus on (and time and money to focus on) self, psychology, and therapy that exists in middle-class culture.[52] It may

15

also be due to different abilities in articulating these concepts or different styles of presenting self to an outsider.

Second, I find *different* class differences for boys and girls. Generally, I find that middle-class boys fare worse than working-class boys in the realms of puberty and sex, and that working-class girls fare worse than middle-class girls. Middle-class boys expressed more uncertainty about puberty and less desire to have sex to establish masculinity. They were also less convinced of the unproblematic nature of their first sexual experiences. Working-class boys were more invested in presenting highly masculine selves. These differences between middle- and working-class boys may be differences in self-presentation. Middle-class boys may be more willing to admit to negative feelings associated with sex and puberty, and middle-class boys were more verbal and talkative than working-class boys were in general.

Working-class girls did not fare worse at puberty, but did in first experiences of sex. Working-class girls are more often in ideal love with male peers, whereas middle-class girls seemed to remain in ideal love with their fathers well into adolescence and did not as often or as quickly pursue ideal love with male peers. Being in ideal love with a boyfriend leads working-class girls to have sex earlier and makes it harder for them to say no to sex they do not want. In addition, there may also be something simply about class that gives middle-class girls more of an ability to say no to sex they do not want. That is, middle-class girls may be more agentic than working-class girls are at the outset. Middle-class girls certainly invest more time and importance in school, sports, and other talents, like art, dance, or music, than working-class girls, who receive less recognition from peers and especially parents for participating in these activities, and this too helps middle-class girls to be more agentic. Finally, sex may be different for middle- and working-class girls because they are interacting with different types of boys. As I have suggested, working-class boys are more interested in being masculine, and sex is one important way of achieving and demonstrating masculinity. Thus, working-class girls may be pressured to have sex more often than middle-class girls, who usually date middle-class boys who are somewhat less eager to have sex than working-class boys.

While I cannot draw conclusions from my data about differential effects of race, ethnicity, and sexual preferences on these processes, there is some literature on these questions. Teens of different racial-ethnic backgrounds also experience puberty and first sexual experiences differently. Nonwhite teens must cope with standards of beauty based on white models, yet black teenage girls may have the advantage of not being as susceptible to feeling fat as white teenage girls when they put on weight as they enter puberty.[53] But there are also similarities across race and ethnicity. Contrary to stereotypes that depict young African-Americans as more "sexually permissive" than young whites,

research finds that "the sexual behaviors of the two groups did not significantly differ."[54] Similarly, other researchers warn us against seeing Asian-
American's reluctance to discuss sexuality in more public ways as asexuality.[55]

Sexual preference also shapes teens' experiences of puberty, first sex, and
self. Interestingly, for gays and lesbians, the younger one is when she or he
comes out the better her/his self-esteem will be. In particular, lesbians who
knew they were gay at an early age were likely to have particularly high self-
esteem in young adulthood.[56] The majority of gay and lesbian teenagers have
also had heterosexual experiences, and similarities among teens' experiences of
body and sexuality seemed to be based on gender rather than on sexual preferences.

> Women, however, lag behind men both in amount of sexual experimen-
> tation and in their age at first same-sex experience; one study, for exam-
> ple, found that lesbians, including even those who already identified
> themselves as lesbian, had their first same-sex sexual experience at age
> twenty-three. Thus, the differences between gay men and lesbians mirror
> the differences between men and women more generally than between
> homosexuals and heterosexuals.[57]

Also, lesbian teens report coercion in heterosexual sex as heterosexual teenage
girls do, but they experience first lesbian sex quite positively.[58]

There are other differences in teen selves as well. Thorne observes a great
variety of sizes in the elementary school children she studied and is amazed at
the different rates of growth among children.[59] During the teen years, for girls
especially, size and height even out somewhat, but differences in growth still
exist. These differences, however, are not evident until one talks to teens. In
my data, among girls of the same age, there were enormous differences in
maturity, social skills, and self-insight. Boys were not the only ones who lacked
insight into themselves; some girls did as well. A striking example comes from
the contrast between two working-class girls whom I interviewed back to
back. Jill was eighteen and Meghan was seventeen. Both were seniors in high
school. Jill shook my hand when I introduced myself to her and again when
she left. She was confident and insightful about herself and her experiences
throughout the interview. At the end of the interview, we talked at length
about her plans for community college and perhaps later college. After Jill left
I met with Meghan. I wrote in my field notes, "Really quiet and self-conscious. She wasn't able to answer many of the questions—asked, 'what do you
mean?' or said, "I don't know" often. Seems much younger than the other girls
I have interviewed so far. Was trying to act grown up, by trying to talk about
the weather, the area, and etc. Seemed very unreflective, her answers more

17

shallow than most of the other girls." These two girls exemplify the very different rates of social growth that exist among teens.

Similarly, there was a fine line between childhood and adolescence for boys as well. Fifteen-year-old Ed had a girlfriend whom he said he was thinking about having sex with soon if he could get her to agree. At the same time that he was setting out on this "adult" or at least adolescent course, he was planning to work as an architect who designed toys for Toys R Us when he graduated from college—a career plan filled with childhood fantasy. After interviewing many teens, it became clear that teens' social growth, like Thorne's children's physical growth, varied enormously both within and between individuals.

COMPROMISES AND STRATEGIES.

I document throughout the book that girls make compromises and adopt a variety of strategies for coping with the gradual loss of agency and sexual subjectivity. Narrative work is a strategy that allows girls to strive for agency and sexual subjectivity. Narrative work is the telling of a story that attempts to reconcile their contradictory feelings and contradictory cultural scripts about "deciding" to have sex. It is a method of balancing what happened, how things are "supposed" to happen, according to cultural and interpersonal scripts, and how one wants them to be. Girls use narrative work to make sense of their first experiences of sex and to construct some feelings of agency or sexual subjectivity when they are feeling very unagentic. (See Chapter Four.)

There are, however, less compromising ways for some girls to achieve some agency and sexual subjectivity. (See Chapter Six.) Middle-class girls often found agency (although not sexual subjectivity) through sports or school or some other special talents or activities. Many of these girls wanted to delay sex until they were older, or they gave sex a secondary role in their lives. Other girls use the strategy of "telling off" boys. These girls derived strength, agency, and sexual subjectivity from resisting boys' sexual advances and claiming that they would not let any boy tell them what to do. Although these girls also told stories of ideal love, their sense of indignation at the thought that they would be taken advantage of kept them from fully investing in ideal love.

Finally, I find the strongest sense of agency and sexual subjectivity in two girls whose mothers were able to facilitate these capacities in their daughters. These girls found much agency in sports and school, but most importantly their mothers recognized their agency and facilitated some sexual subjectivity in their daughters. Each of these mothers helped her daughter develop a sense of knowing her self and doing for herself. These girls put themselves first and thought, with the help of their mothers, about what they wanted and should get from sexual relationships. In this way, these girls expressed the most sexual subjectivity of all the girls in my sample.

"MY HAIR IS MY ACCOMPLISHMENT"

Gender Differences at Puberty

*I was glad when I finally got taller and older. Being
older you just get to do more, go out and stuff.*
    —Joe, a fifteen-year-old working-class boy.

*I didn't know what it [puberty] meant. So am I sup-
posed to be like a woman now? Or what? It seemed
so awkward to be like a little girl with breasts, I
couldn't have both, but I didn't want to be a woman,
but like I didn't, it didn't feel right to me. It felt really awkward, but there wasn't anything to do about it.*
    —Nicole, a fifteen-year-old middle-class girl.

chapter 3

AS THE two above quotes indicate, boys and girls experience puberty very differently. For girls, puberty is characterized by ambivalence about leaving
childhood and anxiety about their new bodies, and these two emotions are
connected. For boys, puberty is characterized by anticipation of adulthood
and by some uncertainty about their new bodies. However, for boys feelings
of agency and a general liking of their new bodies overrides this uncertainty.
At puberty boys are able to take pleasure in their selves and their bodies, while
girls have difficulty doing so. Why is this experience so different for girls and
boys?

   In this chapter I argue that cultural notions of gender and sexuality, cou-
pled with the physiological differences in boys' and girls' development,
account for the differences in emotional experiences of puberty. Leaving
childhood means moving toward adult sexuality, and adult sexuality is gen-

dered. Through puberty boys and girls incorporate these different meanings of sexuality into their selves. Girls come to associate sexuality with danger, shame, and dirt, and boys to associate it with masculinity and adulthood. Why do girls and boys experience puberty differently and how do pubertal events cause girls' and boys' to feel differently about themselves? First, I will examine girls' experiences of puberty and then turn to examine boys' experiences.

GIRLS AND PUBERTAL AMBIVALENCE...

Many girls are ambivalent about their new bodies and about leaving childhood and moving into adulthood. They are unsure about the changes and growth they are experiencing, particularly menarche and breast development. For example, several girls whom I spoke to looked forward to menarche but then felt ambivalence or remorse or regret after they started their periods.[60] Amy, a working-class sixteen-year-old girl said, "I was happy at first 'cause a couple of my friends had already had it, so I was like 'oh when am I going to get mine?' But then I just automatically hated it after it happened." Sharon, who is fifteen years old and middle-class, expressed her ambivalence about the event saying, "I kind of was glad to get it, but then I kind of wasn't. I don't know. I was kind of like waiting for it, so I don't know. It's weird." Some adolescent girls suggest that they are still ambivalent about this bodily change. Heidi, a middle-class girl, said that when she first began menstruating she was "proud of it" but now just turned seventeen she says "if I had my choice I'd never get my period and every time I get my period I curse being a woman."

Other girls expressed this same ambivalence, and some anxiety, when their mothers insisted on discussing their new bodies or their status as women rather than girls. Many girls expressed some resentment toward their mothers for insisting on recognizing the growth they were experiencing. For instance, Andrea, a working-class sixteen-year-old, said that she was "embarrassed" and "felt like an idiot" when her mother told her father and grandparents that she had started her period, and her grandmother congratulated her for being a woman. Other girls felt more than ambivalence. They expressed anxiety and a wish to stay childlike, to cover up or in some way conceal their new bodies, perhaps perpetuated in some by their fathers' insistences that they cover their bodies, as we will examine further in Chapter Five. Kim told me that she was "really self-conscious" about developing breasts and that she "would always try to wear things so that it wouldn't show." Other girls, like fifteen-year-old Nicole, quoted at the beginning of this chapter, explicitly expressed a feeling of wanting to remain a child. Puberty seemed to be changing them into something they did not want to be.

Why do girls have this ambivalence and anxiety about puberty? This wish to stay a child? There are two explanations for this ambivalence and anxiety. First, girls lack knowledge, what I call subjective knowledge, about their bodies, and second, puberty becomes associated with adult female sexuality. The combination of these two social-cultural forces make puberty a difficult experience for girls.

SUBJECTIVE BODY KNOWLEDGE...

Sexuality and a new sexual body are anxiety producing for girls because they often have little subjective knowledge about their own bodies and many times little cognitive knowledge as well. Subjective knowledge is practical, material knowledge from experience, knowledge that usually has emotion behind it. In contrast, cognitive knowledge is learned, rational, thinking, abstracted from experience. Most girls have little subjective knowledge about their bodies and sexuality until (and sometimes not even when) they become adults. Girls reach puberty earlier than boys do. Thus, the fourteen-year-old boys often looked like they could still be in elementary school, whereas many of the fourteen-year-old girls looked to be in their twenties much of this due not simply to their physical maturity but to their work on appearance—jewelry, hair, make-up, clothes.

Working-class girls in this study had less knowledge than the middle-class girls, but neither had enough. Kendra, a particularly articulate middle-class girl with more feminist sensibilities than most of the teenage girls explicitly recognized that girls do not know much about their sexual bodies.

> Okay, one thing that I thought was really nice about using tampons is it in a way forces you to get to know your body. You kind of have to know what you're doing, and I think it does make you a little more comfortable with your body to be able to put a tampon in and out because in a sense I think a pad is like, because it's still outside your body and you're still like not really dealing, it's just like you take this, and okay, you throw it out.

21

Kendra explains that girls will get to know their bodies better if they are "force[d]" to. She sees tampons as a vehicle to subjective body knowledge and body comfort. Boys, as we will see, do not have to be "forced" to get to know their bodies. Unfortunately, most girls are not as interested in their bodies as Kendra. Most girls, especially working-class girls, seem afraid of their sexual bodies, afraid of exploring them, afraid of what they might find. It was not uncommon to hear stories like Jodi, a working-class seventeen-year-old, and Danielle told me.

> I never have [looked at my genitals]. Once I started using tampons I was just like "Oops, I guess that's the place where everything happens." I never looked. I know one girl who said in real discreet privacy, "Once when I

was little I took a mirror and looked down there so I could see what it looked like."

—Jodi

Have you ever been to the gynecologist?
No and I want to but I'm afraid to. I don't want to like (spreads her arms apart), you know (giggling) that's gross! I don't know if I should have a man or a woman. I want to go just to make sure nothing's like, that I don't have any like…birth defects inside me or something, I don't know.

—Danielle

Jodi's and Danielle's fears of their own sexual bodies are even more disturbing in light of the fact that they were both sexually active. Their boyfriends were allowed more access to their bodies than they allowed themselves.

This lack of knowledge about sexuality and one's changing body can have disturbing results. As other researchers have found, the amount of information one has about menstruation at menarche can greatly influence one's experience of it.[61] For example, Stephanie and Jill had no knowledge of menstruation when they started their periods. Stephanie said,

I was babysitting and I just like got home, and I just like was screaming! 'Cause, umm, I ran upstairs and I didn't know what it was 'cause I got home late one night, and I was just going to the bathroom, and I ran upstairs 'cause I didn't know what it was…and then she's [my mother's] like, "Don't worry about it, it's just your period."

Jill, who is also working-class, at eighteen can still vividly remember her first period because it was such a frightening incident for her.

I can remember [starting my period] distinctly 'cause that was a nightmare for me. My parents had just left to go out to dinner, and I waved to them out the window, and they drove away. And then I was going to take a bath or a shower, I can't remember which. I went into the bathroom and I looked down and there was blood and I was just like "What is that?" I thought I was bleeding to death. I was flipping out. I was crying. I had to wait about twenty minutes before I thought they would be at the restaurant they were at. I had to call them up. She [my mom] was just like "Don't worry about it. We'll be right home." So she came home. She was like "I guess I should tell you." I was like "Yeah! That would be appropriate right now!"

Neither Stephanie nor Jill had cognitive or subjective knowledge about menarche. Stephanie felt fear and confusion. Jill describes first feeling deep fear about what was happening to her and then that fear turning into anger and resentment at her mother for not having better prepared her.[62] This anger was expressed at her mother not only in this context, but throughout her discussions of puberty.

However, even when girls have cognitive knowledge, a lack of subjective knowledge alone can cause them to feel confused or anxious. For example, Heather, not knowing what her vagina feels like or how it works is afraid both of feeling too much (pain) and of feeling nothing in her vagina when she uses a tampon. Her mother and friends had told her it would not hurt, that she would not feel anything, but by her own logical thinking, and with little subjective knowledge about her vagina, it did not make sense that she would feel nothing with something inside of her body. Notice in her discussion of this that her doctor probably enhances this fear because he suggests that there is an age that is too young to use a tampon.

> Well, I got my period when I was real young. Just turned eleven I think, and umm, so the doctor said it wasn't a good idea for me to use tampons at that young age so I used pads, until I got to be—how old are you when you start high school?—fourteen? So for three years I used pads and all my friends were starting to use tampons so I thought, I have to do this. My mom had showed me how to do it, but it was something that I was really scared of…*I thought it would hurt or I thought it would…I guess I thought it would hurt and I thought it would be uncomfortable, and I couldn't imagine how something could be inside of you and you could not feel it.*

The idea of having something inside one's body that will hurt or that one cannot feel made Heather anxious about her body. Although this anxiety is psychological, it is a cultural phenomenon that produces it. Girls are culturally denied knowledge about their bodies, particularly their genitals. Lerner suggests that this knowledge is denied girls from early childhood.[63] Whereas parents often name boys' genitals—for example, wee-wee, pee-pee, or unit—they are much less likely to give girls specific names for their genitals. Girls' genitals often become generalized to "down there" or "private parts." Rarely do girls have specific names that distinguish between vagina, clitoris, vulva.[64]

Physiology combined with missing cognitive and/or subjective knowledge about one's body also causes girls to feel like they have little control over their bodies. Some girls expressed what sounded like a sense that their body was out of control, or betraying them. Feeling out of control contributes to girls' general anxiety at puberty.

23

> A lot of my friends didn't have it [when I got mine]. I remember that. A
> lot of them didn't. It kind of sucked...*I was like "Aaahhhhhh, my body!?"*
>
> —Amanda, working-class fifteen-year-old.

Other girls simply expressed that they did nothing, and their period "just
started." Other researchers similarly find that women describe menarche as
something that happens to them rather than something that is a part of
them.[65] The girls whom I interviewed also describe menarche as disconnected from themselves, as something that happens out of the blue.

> I can remember it was in August and I woke up and I had pains, so I went
> to the bathroom, and *there it was*.
>
> —Amy

> I got it at camp! I just woke up, and *it was there*. It was awful! There was
> like no running water. There was like an outhouse. I slept over like with
> one of my friends. They have a camp way up in the mountains, a cabin.
> I got it like the day we were gonna leave. There was no pads or anything
> like that. I was like "Oh, I want to go home!"
>
> —Meghan

Meghan's description of menarche reveals one more aspect of puberty that
causes some girls anxiety about their new body and about leaving childhood.
Girls have more anxiety if pubertal events do not occur according to a normative cultural scenario. This is true mainly for menstruation. A girl is, according to a normative cultural scenario, supposed to begin her period at home,
with a supportive, informative mother, with knowledge of what is happening
to her, with pads (or occasionally tampons) available. It is clear such a normative cultural story exists because when telling me about menarche girls
(explicitly and implicitly) assess their own experiences compared to this cultural story about menstruation. Also, descriptions of the films about menstruation that girls saw were full of these prescriptions. Normative cultural stories
about pubertal events probably vary by class, religion, race, or even region of
the country.[66] We also know from previous research that the experience of
menarche varies according to how well prepared girls are with information
about menarche before the event.[67]

The girls whose experiences most closely followed this normative story had
much less anxiety than girls' experiences that did not. For example, Meghan's
experience, quoted above, resembled what many girls feared—being without
their mothers, being away from home, and without "pads or anything." In particular, many girls feared starting their periods at school. This is more true for
early developers than for late developers who were better equipped—materi-

ally and psychologically. In Simon and Gagnon's terms, the more a girl has to improvise, tinker, and scriptwrite the more anxiety she has about the event.[68]

Also, being an early developer is violating the cultural story in and of itself. Early developing girls, we know, fare worst at puberty.[69] Girls who are early developers suffer because they look older and more sexual than their peers at an early age. This often results in teasing from others and feelings of self-consciousness. Thorne found that even teachers commented on the girls who "had their development" in elementary school.[70]

Being an on-time developer, that is, being "in sync" with one peers, is best for girls.[71] Several girls indicated this to me. Amy said, "You know, like if one of their friends says 'I got my first bra.' Then they have to run home and tell their mother 'Oh, so-and-so got her first bra. When can I get mine?' You know. And the same thing with periods like 'So-and-so started her period, when can I start mine?' You know." Similarly, Kristen told me, "And people in middle school if you're a girl, you really, really want your period if you don't have it. And how much pubic hair you have in middle school. You know, 'cause you get unchanged and if you don't have any…stuff like that. You want to be like your friends and you want to be noticed by the guys."

Girls who fared best at menarche followed the cultural scenario to a tee, as did Diana, a working-class fifteen-year-old. Diana told me simply and proudly, "I went to the bathroom and then I told my mother, and she sent me flowers! I was proud, and she was happy." Following this cultural story provides girls a feeling of safety and security for two reasons. Having a supportive mother and being at home makes the event easier, but also, following the cultural story in itself feels safe, normal, and expected.

For one girl, however, this cultural prescription made her experience more difficult. Kelly, a middle-class seventeen-year-old, told me that when she had her first period she knew what it was, knew what to do, and thought it was not a big deal. However, she did not tell her mother she had started her period the first time. She did not need to, did not want to. When she had her second period, she felt like she *had* to tell her mother because that was what one was "supposed to do" at menarche. Kelly agonized over how to and when to tell her. However, when she finally did tell her mother, she pretended that it was her first period, and she let her mother go through the ritual of treating her like it was her first period—getting her tampons and pads, asking if she was okay, asking if she had cramps, letting her stay home from school. The hard part of menarche for this girl was not the actual experience of menstruation but having to enact the cultural story of menarche, then "feeling guilty" about "lying" to her mother.

Finally, some girls are denied control of their bodies outright by parents and other adults who insist on supervising teenage girls' sexual bodies. When girls feel out of control of their own bodies, it causes them to feel powerless. Tracy,

25

a working-class seventeen-year-old, told me the following story when I asked her if she has ever been to the gynecologist.

> Yeah. My mother tricked me into that one. She told me I was going to get a physical. I was really fatigued at the time. I was concerned about it, and I asked her to take me to the doctor. So instead of taking me to the doctor, she told me she was taking me to get a physical, and she took me to the gynecologist. I didn't even realize what I was doing until I was on the table itself and they were looking. Yeah, she did that because...I started being sexually active when I was fourteen, and she took me when I was about fifteen, and she wanted to make sure I was okay. I guess. I don't really know what her motive was. Yeah, she had tricked me into that one.
> *So were you scared?!*
> Yeah, yeah, I was...I didn't know what was going on. They didn't tell me. They just went in and did it. I didn't even know what they did. I was like what are you doing. It was...I remember there was a mobile of seagulls hanging from the ceiling and they just said relax and pretend you're at the beach. I just remember I told them that if I was at the beach I wouldn't be sitting sprawled up all like this on the sand. Yeah, it was scary.

This case of parental (and physician) control over a teenage girls' sexual body may (or may not) be a more extreme case. But in many smaller ways, from withholding information to insisting on knowing when a girl begins menstruating, parents and other adults maintain some control over girls' sexual bodies.

PUBERTY AND ADULT FEMALE SEXUALITY...

Now I turn to the second explanation for girls' anxiety and ambivalence about puberty. Pubertal events—menarche, shaving, breast development—evoke cultural meanings about men's and women's bodies, especially their sexual bodies. The forms and types of body images (and self-images) that girls construct certainly vary by race, ethnicity, class, religion, and other social-cultural factors.[72] Taboos about bodies and images of women's bodies vary by these factors. Also women of oppressed groups must cope with beauty and body standards constructed by the dominant group, as well as by their own culture. Cherrie Moraga, for example, writes of her struggle of coming into her own sexuality in Catholic and Chicano culture and in a white-dominated world. Her images of body and sexuality were influenced by her Mexican heritage and religious symbolism. These images included one of Malinche, the woman who "fucked the white man who conquered the Indian peoples of Mexico and destroyed their culture."[73] She is considered a traitor to the race. In trying to establish her sexual identity (as a lesbian) Moraga encountered this image again and again. Also, in her adolescence images of her body and sexuality came from Catholicism. Moraga writes,

> In my 'craziness' I wrote poems describing myself as a centaur: half animal/half-human, hairy-rumped and cloven-hoofed, como el diablo. The symbols emerged from a deeply Mexican and Catholic place.[74]

Moraga's experience is an example of the ways in which girls structure their sense of body and sexuality in the context of particular social and cultural milieus. The content of one's sense of self as a sexual being, subject or not, is always particular to one's personal social, cultural, racial, ethnic, class, psychological, familial, background.

In general, puberty, for the girls in my sample, became associated with sexuality, and sexuality and the female sexual body became associated with dirtiness, shame, taboo, danger, and objectification. As girls internalized these meanings, they began to feel bad about their new bodies and themselves. Below I examine each of these associations and how girls incorporate them and experience them.

First, how does puberty become connected to sexuality? At puberty people, especially parents, start to talk to children about sex, even if inadvertently. Often when trying to convey information about puberty and changing bodies, parents and teachers add a partial subtext about sex and sexuality. They make connections, explicit and implicit, between puberty and sexuality.

27

> *Did your parents talk to you about puberty?*
> She [my mother] comes home from a meeting and she says like "Five girls in this class are pregnant," and she says something. I'm like, "I don't care. It's not me. You don't have to talk to me." 'Cause she already has a lot.
> —Sharon

> When I asked my mom about periods, well, like she like besieged me with all these sex books and she had like *Let's Talk about S-E-X* and *What's Happening to My Body*. And she like forced me to read them.
> —Nicole

In Thorne's observation of official sex education—a film on menstruation—in a fifth-grade elementary school classroom, she found that amid girls' giggling about periods and boys' "sperms" the teacher launched into an explanation of gender relations. Mrs. Sorenson said,

> I realize it's different seeing it with the boys; don't you think it's better if the boys know and can understand? If they don't understand, they might

> be afraid of it. I live in a family of men; I have two boys and a forty-seven-year-old boy, my husband; men are like boys, so I can tell you, boys are unsure of themselves; that's why they are nervous themselves...Now we know it's okay for boys to cry, to say what they want to say; we didn't used to think that. The person you should marry should be your best friend.[75]

A few minutes later Mrs. Sorenson told the girls she did not want them to talk about the film or its subject on playground. Thus, a lesson about menstruation teaches girls about gender relations, marriage, and hidden amongst all that, that boys might be afraid of menstruation, that it is something scary and not to be talked about.

Depending on how information about menstruation, gender relations, and sex was distorted by the girls' absorption of it or how parents, teachers, or peers convey it, girls begin to understand cultural ideas about sex and link them to puberty in a variety of ways. This is especially true of menarche. Lee (1994) suggests "...menarche is an important time when young women become inserted and insert themselves into the dominant patterns of sexuality."[76] For example, for many girls starting one's period meant that now one could get pregnant, now one would get pregnant, now one could have sex, now one could not have sex. Jill, a working-class eighteen-year-old told me,

> A lot of girls that I hung around with thought as soon as you got your period at any moment you could spontaneously be pregnant. So you know, if you were making out with a guy, you know, the big question was, "Oh my God, I made out with someone. Can I be pregnant?" I think that's a big one. When kids start getting their periods, they hear all this stuff like "When you're not pregnant you get this." So they're like, "How do I get pregnant?" and stuff like that. It's scary.

In a more extreme case, Audrey, a middle-class sixteen-year-old, thought that she "had to" start having sex, that is, it was required.

> I was really upset [when I started my period]. I was crying. I remember it was on my birthday and I was like "God hates me." Just something about me I didn't want to have that stuff start happening to me...Well, you want to know, it sounds really irrational, but I do remember one thought I had. *I thought it meant that I had to start having sex,* and I felt really weird, and I felt really rushed. I was in seventh grade, I mean, I was a really late bloomer [socially], and I didn't even start talking to guys until eighth or ninth grade. I was really shy and I remember I was like I can't really talk to any guys today 'cause they'll know, they'll know. And I

remember being in homeroom that day and thinking "Oh no, I can't face anyone that day."

Thus, puberty, especially menarche, becomes associated with adult female sexuality.

DIRT, SHAME, TABOO, AND DANGER...

Menarche and menstruation are also particularly laden with associations to dirtiness and to excrement. Culturally, we think menstruation is dirty.[77] Girls learn these cultural meanings from peers, parents, siblings, advertising, and boys' joking.

> My sister told me about using tampons. My sister is a lot older than I am. So at first I didn't like the idea of having to go anywhere near touching myself. I thought it was sick! But my sister was like, *"You can wear diapers all your life* or you can wear whatever you want and wear these."
>
> —Jill

Jill learns from her sister that a pad is like a diaper—something soiled and shameful to be wearing. Her sister scolds her about wearing pads as a parent might scold a child about still wearing diapers—shaming her with "Do you want to wear diapers all your life?"

Knowledge, conscious or not, of the cultural idea that menstruation is unclean can also combine with girls' cursory, limited knowledge of their own bodies and leads them to associate menstruation with other excretory functions and think their bodies are "disgusting."

29

> I was in fifth grade at least. I started real early. I got it at home and I didn't know what it was really. I did sort of. After awhile, I was, "Ma, I think I got my period." She's like, *"Well where is it, in the middle, in the front, or in the back?"* I'm like, "In the middle." She's like, "Well, I think you got it." And I hated it 'cause then I didn't wear tampons and that really sucked. It was like yuck.
>
> —Danielle

Even Kristen, who was eagerly awaiting the arrival of her period, did not know immediately that she was menstruating.

> I went into the bathroom, and *I thought I shit my pants (laughing),* and then, I was like "Holy shit!" and then my best friend was in there, and she was like, "You got your period didn't you!" And I was like "Ooooh yeaaaah." And I was like "Oh my God, I bet you this is it."

The girls whom I interviewed gave only negative descriptions of their menstruating bodies. Their bodies made them feel "yuck," or "sick," or as if they had "shit [their] pants." This association with excrement and with shame make many girls feel badly about their sexual/menstruating bodies.

Working-class girls also expressed what sounded like menstrual taboos. Several working-class girls said they would not go swimming or were told they could not go swimming when they were menstruating. Other girls said that they could not wear shorts or white clothes. Another said she did not like to dance. Others said, suggesting it was a rule, that they "go to the bathroom more, like to check to make sure there's nothing on my shorts." Finally, Meghan exclaimed in the course of discussing how she felt about menstruating, "Sometimes you just have to sit and stay away from things!" These modern menstrual taboos limit working-class girls' activities and keep them focused on and worried about their bodies.

Menarche also often makes girls feel ashamed or as if they have done something wrong. Esther and I had a conversation where she explained that menarche was a big crisis in her life. She felt that becoming a woman was "a nightmare," something to be frightened of and something to be punished for. As we talked, six years after she began menstruating, anxiety and incredulity sounded in her voice as she told me about her experience.

> *How old were you [when you started your period]?*
> I was in sixth grade, so eleven or twelve. That was a scary experience. At first my mom thought it was like…*the beginning of a new world*. She told everybody her daughter was *a woman now*. I was really embarrassed. I can remember that. That was a nightmare.
> *Do you remember how you felt after the first few days, over the next few weeks?*
> I thought *the world had come to an end*. I felt like *"Oh, God's punishing me or something." I'd go to school and come right home*. I wouldn't tell anyone about it. That was horrible. Then I heard one girl say—the first time I'd ever heard the phrase—"Oh my God, I'm ragging." I was like "I don't know what you mean." She said "My period, my period, I'm having my period." I said, "Oh you are? You mean I'm not the only one suffering alone?" At first I thought the whole world had come to an end 'cause I didn't under…my mom like didn't go into depth. She just said, "This is your period. You get it once a month."

Esther's mother thinks menarche is the beginning of "a new world," her daughter's womanhood. However, Esther does not share her mother's joy in this new world, but rather experiences her period as "the end of the world," that is the world of childhood. According to her mother she was "a woman now." Esther also fears the new world that her mother proposes she has entered, the world of adult womanhood and adult female sexuality. To Esther, it feels like a world in which she is being punished by "God" or "something." In fact, it sounds like Esther punished herself. She goes "to school and come[s] right home." This is a punishment a parent would bestow on a child—"You will go to school and come straight home." Instead Esther grounds herself until she begins to realize that other girls are menstruating as she is, that she has not done something wrong by entering this "new world" of adulthood.

Puberty and emerging sexuality also becomes associated with danger. In particular, girls learn about the dangerous aspects of sexuality when they develop breasts. Thorne (1993), citing Frigga Haug, writes, "'Female breasts are never innocent,' for as soon as they appear, they signal sexuality."[78] Breasts attract attention from men and boys, and breasts provoke warnings about boys and sex from parents and other adults. When girls develop breasts, especially if they are early developers, they immediately know that their body is changing shape because they see others recognizing this. In particular, men and boys "notice" girls' breasts and comment on them. Girls feel that boys judge them and their sexuality when they "notice" their breasts. This finding is quite different from that of previous research that suggests that girls (aged nine-to-eleven) perceive breast development as private and therefore that breast development is associated with "positive peer relationships and with adjustment."[79] Perhaps because Brooks-Gunn and Warren's research examined nine-to-eleven-year-olds, the social context of development had not become as sexualized as it is for teens.[80] In particular, boys, according to the girls in my sample, suggest bigger breasts mean a girl is more sexually available or adventurous. Many girls, especially working-class girls, said defiantly and frustratedly, things like Wendy, Sondra, Jill, and Jen did.

31

I was self-conscious [when I developed breasts]. I still am. I don't know. It's just the boys. Some of them, how they react and stuff, just like *if you're bigger you're better* and stuff like that, some of the boys, I know some. It's aggravating.

—Wendy

I was really self-conscious 'cause I developed them early, I think it was like fifth grade, and you know guys sometimes would say things.

—Sondra

When I started to get them and now that I have them, I wish I didn't have them 'cause they're a pain. 'Cause like you have to worry about them when you get dressed in the morning. If you don't…well, I'm just, I mean, I am self-conscious about my chest. I wish I was little again where

> you know, no one really worried about it and guys didn't really care as
> much and all that stuff. You know now it's the first thing they check out!
>
> —Jill

> Umm, it was scary 'cause I developed a lot faster than anyone else did.
> But now, there are people bigger than me.
> *Do you remember what was scary about it?*
> 'Cause no one looked like me, you know. And all the guys were starting
> to notice me and they weren't noticing anyone else, you know. So it was
> kind of scary. But I was kind of tough, a tough girl, so *they knew they could-*
> *n't get away with anything with me.*
>
> —Jen

This constant objectification of their bodies and selves causes girls to feel self-conscious. Boys' and others' judgments make their new sexual bodies seem displayed and potentially dangerous or "scary."

Having their bodies objectified, particularly their breasts, not only makes girls self-conscious and scared, but also makes them feel ashamed of their own and other women's bodies. As a result, girls often want their bodies to be different. With respect to breasts, this usually means that flat chested girls want to have larger breasts and large chested girls want to have smaller breasts. Tiffany expressed disgust and shame at breasts in general, and in particular the desire to change her own body. With real disdain in her voice she said, "I didn't want to be too big. I think that looks [*makes a face*]…I don't, I don't understand why people get breast implants, I think that looks disgusting. I'd probably like to be more skinny in that area,…like running, I just don't like it."

For working-class girls, breast development evokes a sense of sex as dangerous in another way as well. As children reach puberty parents treat them differently. Boys often receive more freedom as they look older, and girls often receive less because they look sexual.[81] As girls develop breasts and look more sexual to parents, working-class parents, especially fathers, begin to warn their daughters about men and sex. I asked all the interviewees if their parents gave them advice on dating or relationships, and I discovered that warnings were the only kind of advice girls could remember getting from their parents. Jen, who prided herself on being tough anyway, said, "My mother just says, 'They're not good enough for you. If a guy ever tries anything just remember your karate.' Things like that." I asked her what her father had to say about it, and she replied, "Just 'if a guy ever lays a hand on you and you don't want to, just kick him where it counts.'" Similarly, Meghan and Amanda said,

32

[My father says] Never…never let a guy take advantage of you or um if they ever say anything about hitting, about hitting girls just don't have anything to do with them because he's gonna do the same thing to you. My father used to say that too. "If you ever meet a guy whose father, whose father beats up his mother, he's gonna do the same thing to you 'cause he's gonna think it's okay." Like because if he sees his dad do it he's gonna try it on you. Don't date anybody that has that problem.

—Meghan

My father, just…Well, they both just told me to like to look out and not to put up with anything and stuff like that. You know to be careful and you know, stuff like that.

—Amanda

These warnings help to make boys, sex, and girls' own bodies seem "scary" and dangerous to girls. Boys did not receive similar warnings. They usually said that their parents did not give them advice at all or that sometimes their mothers would tell them only that they were wearing the right or wrong clothes to go out.

There are some exceptions to girls' fear of a new sexual body. A grown up body is desirable for *some* girls in *some* contexts. Late developers and girls who are more vigorously pursuing femininity (the two seem related) often find menarche and breasts desirable. Sometimes these girls also feel as if they look like "little girls" to others. One late developer told me, "I think I have a pug nose and chubby cheeks. I have a baby face…I look like I'm about twelve years old." Another said that people looked at her "like a little kid." These girls often feel left behind by their peers who have already passed through these pubertal rites. They worry about confirming their adult status and femininity and want to shed their identity as a child. This is especially true as girls move from junior high to high school. Michelle, a working-class eighteen-year-old "couldn't wait" to start her period.

Yeah, umm, I was, it [my period] was like the first week of school freshmen year and every, like, a lot of people had it, and I didn't have it and like guys just wicked…I just wanted it so bad, just to feel older. You know your freshmen year is pretty sad.

Kelly and Kristen both wanted to develop breasts. Kelly, a middle-class seventeen-year-old said, "I mean like freshmen year I stuffed my bra to fit into my prom dress, umm, you know. I still do sometimes when nobody's like really watching." Kristen, a working-class sixteen-year-old, who was also a late developer, said excitedly, "I remember I wanted them when I was younger. I

33

was like 'Yes! I want boobs.' I don't know why, to be like a woman, I guess."
Kristen's entire interview was animated with details like these. She was much
more positive about puberty and sexuality in general and continued her story
about her discovering the importance of breasts to boys and herself.

> I didn't wear a bra until seventh grade, and I picked up this awesome
> eighth grader at a dance, and he felt my back, and I didn't have a bra on,
> and so then I started wearing one after that. I had a little boobs my fresh-
> men and sophomore year but they really took shape, I mean, I went from
> an A to a C in like three months [Junior year when I went on the pill].
> So I remember I was happy because my mom and sister both have them,
> and I think they're so feminine. I was happy to get them, and I'd take the
> boobs and gain weight than be thin with no boobs. I only feel self-con-
> scious like if you wear something, and there are things you can't wear, but
> I felt more self-conscious about not having them and having a guy go up
> my shirt than now.

Again, these girls are the exception. Most girls did not experience menarche
and breast development so positively.

One thing all girls felt strongly about without exception was the objectification of their entire bodies and the judgments about their weight and size.
Becoming an adult woman is associated with objectification and causes girls
to feel self-conscious, like they are scrutinized objects. Girls begin to associate
adult female bodies with objectification as they develop breasts, but they also
see that boys, and often other girls, demean girls bodies in general, not just
their breasts. Heather angrily and vividly recalled this incident at her school
just a few days before our interview.

> I think that bodies are such a big issue with females because males make
> such a big issue of it. I was at a volleyball game the other day and the team
> that we were playing, um, was wearing like those volleyball uniforms...It
> looks like the bottom of a bathing suit, so it looks like you're playing in
> underwear. And, umm, all the guys, you know, in the stands were judging
> them and making fun of them, and they were like "Oh my God, look at
> that one, she's so fat!" or like "If I was that fat I'd never get into some-
> thing like that." I think it's just, you pick on what you hear guys saying
> about other girls and you assume that they're saying similar things about
> you.

Incidents like this one highlight the scrutiny girls' bodies, and especially their
weight, are under. The sum of all of these associations of girls' pubertal bodies
to sexuality and then to dirt, shame, danger, objectification—have two results

34

which in turn affect girls' selves. First, girls dislike their bodies and second, girls come to feel like objects, not like subjects who can act. Let me examine where these two feelings—the feeling of bodily dislike and feeling like an object—lead girls.

FEELINGS OF BODILY DISLIKE...

Early childhood may lay the ground work for women and girls to have an internal dislike of their bodies, but cultural norms, especially at adolescence, specify the content of that dislike as feeling fat.[82] Weight, diets, and eating disorders are a significant part of teenage girl culture. I found this as I talked to a few girls who were less caught up in it than the others. For example, Samantha, a middle-class sixteen-year-old, described her appearance and in doing so said she was not like all the others girls who worry "too much" about being fat, "I guess like my stomach is like, it's like if I ran more. I wish it would be flatter and that I don't know...It's not like [meaning I'm not like] everybody else who runs around "Oh, I'm so fat." I just know if I worked out more or if I did sit-ups or something..." Similarly, Kristen said, "Almost every girl in this school says they're overweight and have about ten things they want to change about themselves. They all want to look like Cindy Crawford or..." She had thought about this aspect of girl culture and discussed it with her friends at length.

> Well, let's put it this way, I'm not gonna like be bulimic or something like half my class is or change me just to impress other people, that's not where I'm at. I'd rather just...I'm happy with myself, you know. Losing weight isn't...I'm not going to do something to make me unhappy to be happy. I have a group of friends called the Girlies, and it's like twenty-two of us and we all hang around, and they all compete so bad it's ridiculous. And like last year me and my friend were just talking, and we had a list of a party, who was invited, and it was all of us and we just went through and picked out how many people were anorexic and bulimic out of all of them and five weren't out of twenty-two! It's pathetic! It's really pathetic!
>
> *Wow, that's a lot.*
>
> It is and umm. I mean, it's gotten better this year because so many people had so many problems last year, and it's just wicked competition to be the best and look the skinniest and look...this image that people have, that guys have...'cause girls are so insecure! Oh I don't want to go off but...It's sad.

35

These girls' observations of their peers are supported by what most girls said when I interviewed them. As teenagers, just past the height of puberty, the girls

I interviewed, generally, have a tremendous dislike of their bodies. In fact, girls, in general, do not like their bodies at all. This observation is born out in the literature on weight, body, and appearance that finds that girls are much more negative about their bodies than boys.[83] There are, however, variations by race. A recent study finds that African-American girls are much more satisfied with their bodies than white girls.[84] While 90% of white girls are *dissatisfied* with their bodies, 70% of African-American girls are *satisfied* with theirs. African-American girls were more likely to talk about "making what you've got work" than talk about dieting. Cultural differences in beauty standards and in media representations may explain this difference. However, this does not mean that African-American girls are free from the struggle with normative beauty standards. Blonde hair and blue eyes are still the icon of female beauty in American culture.[85]

Every girl I interviewed with the exception of one said her body or a part of it was too big or too fat.[86] (All the girls in my sample, although a range of shapes and sizes, appeared to me to be well within average body size.) The only class difference in feeling fat is that middle-class girls, who have more feminist knowledge and a better critique of beauty standards, do not express the feeling as strongly. Here are some examples of feeling fat or too big from a lesser to greater degree.

> I wouldn't mind being a little thinner, but I'm not going on a diet.
>
> —Heidi

> I go through phases where I don't like my weight. Then other days it's fine. But, like if somebody says something negative, I'll think about that for like a week on end.
>
> —Diana

> I'm kinda fat, just sort of.
>
> —Juliana

> I think I'm wide. My hips, I hate my hips and my butt and thighs. I'm huge from like here [waist] down. (Sighs.) It's a pain. I want to get in shape. I don't know how. It's hard. It's gonna kill me.
>
> —Danielle

> *What do you daydream about?*
> Being skinny!
>
> —Amanda

These girls used many strategies in order not to "look fat." Some claimed they wore tight clothes in order to appear thinner, while others said they wore loose clothes for the same effect. Ellen wore tampons instead of pads because "I think pads are so repulsive, and I have a big butt anyway, and I don't want to make it bigger." However, most often this pervasive dislike of their own bodies compels girls to try to change their bodies through dieting.

Dieting, a normative cultural practice, makes girls dislike their *selves* as well as their bodies, because they so often "fail" at it. Silberstein et al. suggest that "feeling fat has become synonymous with feeling bad."[87] In particular, feeling fat invokes shame. "In a state of shame, the entire self is the object of denigration: the ashamed person understands herself to be bad."[88] We clearly see the feeling of shame when girls describe trying to become thin. Meghan, who spoke softly and seemed uncomfortable throughout much of the interview said,

> I went on like a Weight Watchers, and I lost a lot of weight but then I started gaining it back. 'Cause I was down to like 120 pounds, but then I started gaining it back. I put it on. But I'm like right in the middle now. I want to loose like about fifteen pounds. It's hard. It really gets me down…I get discouraged.

Similarly, Nicole explained how diets never worked for her, although she often wished they would, and she was always on the look out for new ways to lose weight.

> I did the thing where you're sick, and you lose a lot of weight, and you're like "Starvation equals skinny! (Claps her hands together) Good idea!" You know, it's hard to say 'cause I never stuck by any diet, and I wouldn't lose any weight. I'd be dieting and dieting and nothing happened, and then I'd get really upset and "Oh, you're a bad person and you're not doing this right." I was never into bulimia and I never starved myself for a long period of time, but the temptation definitely was there. I remember it actually—they showed us a bulimia video to try to make us deter from it and I thought "What a good idea."

As Nicole begins to indicate, girls have a definition of dieting that is frightening and that sets them up to fail and to feel bad about themselves. Middle-class girls make distinctions between dieting and starving, probably because they have been better educated about it in school health programs (although Nicole suggests such education may not work). There is a fine line between the practices and feelings of these girls and those with actual diagnosed eating disorders. Silberstein et al. propose that eating disorders lie on a continuum

37

with the "normative discontent" that most women experience about their bodies.[89] These teen girls' "normative discontent" is closer to the eating disorder end of the continuum than is adult women's "normative discontent."[90]

Working-class girls' view of dieting is most extreme. They equate dieting with not eating at all, or at least eating very little. For this reason, these girls said apologetically that they did not diet because they "had" to eat, as if there was something wrong with them. For example, Amanda said, "Well I did go on a diet, but it only lasted like two weeks. I just don't. I can't…I have to eat. I just can't go without eating." When I asked Valerie if she had ever dieted, she replied apologetically. "Well not diet. But I've cut down a lot. I cut down and watch what I eat. I try not to eat so much anymore, and maybe if I'm hungry I have a salad. I don't diet to the point I starve myself, I've tried that but I can't do it. I like food too much." Finally, Danielle said she had dieted but that it was hard. She confessed, "I went on a diet like last summer, and I had like ice cream with hot fudge on it! I couldn't handle it!"

As this data suggests, dieting causes girls to feel as if they have no will, no control, no agency in themselves. They feel "discouraged," like a "bad person," like they "can't do it" and unable to "handle it." So, girls' dislike of their bodies often becomes a dislike of the self when the diet fails. Bodily dislike is transformed into a general dislike of self because they cannot change their bodies. Finally, dieting is not the only way that girls attempt to change their bodies. They try everything from new hairstyles and clothes to plastic surgery.[91]

There are exceptions to this general bodily dislike. One girl, but only one, said she did like her body and appearance and did not qualify her answer at all. Kelly was middle-class, seventeen, blonde, blue-eyed, thin, and ideally cute. She knew that these looks were culturally valued and would help her. Her looks made her confident and gave her a sense of entitlement to be herself that many girls did not have.

> I think I lucked out because I like the way I look. It gives me a lot of confidence. I know when I walk down the street there are guys that turn around, and you know, that's not like my whole sense of self…Sometimes getting ready to go out with my friends or something I can look in the mirror and say "All right!" And what that does for me, it really makes me confident that I can, that I don't have to deal with any of the jerks that a lot of people think they have to deal with. I don't have to go out with people who treat me badly, I don't have to stand for it. And that really, in my social life I don't drink, I don't smoke, I don't do drugs, and I just feel like I don't need to alter my personality to have a good time.

Kelly likes her body. However, she still experiences body and self as objects in relation to men's "gaze," although not in the negative way most other girls did.

Finally, another exception to the issue of appearance was a girl for whom it was not an issue either way. Sara, a sixteen-year-old whose family was from Hong Kong, said she didn't worry about the same things her friends did—like appearance and boys—because she had "other things" to worry about. She told me at length about her concern for her extended family that was still Hong Kong and what would happen to them when Hong Kong reverted to China in 1997. Sara knew so much more about politics than most teens and her concerns were so much larger than most other teens', her interview was a striking contrast to the other interviews. Sara's experience suggests that there are many ways of thinking about self, and the type of interview I constructed elicited a particularly western (even American) version of (a female) self.

FEELING LIKE AN OBJECT...

But, above all, the lie to which the adolescent girl is condemned is that she must pretend to be an object, and a fascinating one, when she senses herself as an uncertain, dissociated being, well aware of her blemishes.

—Simone de Beauvoir, *The Second Sex.*

Feeling watched and judged solidifies girls' feeling that they are objects. This feeling/fearing that she is an object is present from early childhood,[92] and thus partially explains why girls feel so awful when men look at, judge, and objectify them. It confirms their fears. They discover in the course of their daily lives, that they *are* objects because others treat them as such. Thus, when I asked girls, especially working-class girls, to describe themselves or asked "Tell me about yourself," they described their bodies and had a difficult time describing any other aspects of who they were.

39

> *Tell me about yourself. How would you describe yourself?*
> Ummmm. I'm not sure. Ah…Um, dark hair, brown eyes…I don't know like…
>
> —Ellen

> *Tell me about yourself. How would you describe yourself?*
> Like…(pauses)…like?
> *Personality wise, what you like or dislike to do, anything about yourself.*
> I hate my short stubby legs. What do you mean like?
>
> —Elaine

Tell me about yourself. How would you describe yourself?
Umm…short, I don't know. I like to get involved in things.

—Stephanie

As a result of being "noticed" and objectified by others, girls also come to objectify their own bodies. They treat their bodily selves as objects they have taken apart. Their bodies become a detailed list of the minute flaws and attributes they possess. Both middle-class and working-class girls do this.

I like my hair and my eyes, and my freckles make me unique. And my height's pretty cool. I like my nose. I don't like the shape of my body. The shape of it, that's pretty much it.

—Jen

My fingers are like wicked bony. I hate that. I hate it. They're not bad now, but like if we take pictures and I'm like this [she leans her head on her fist to show that you can see the bones in her hand]. They're like that. It just shows up wicked bad on this side.

—Juliana

Yeah, I like it [my body] okay. Just like little physical characteristics, I don't like. Like the little bump on my nose, um, I have a mark here [points to her chin] that looks like a pen mark, just like little things.

—Valerie

How would you describe the way that you look?
Long brown hair, straight long brown hair, except in the rain it gets curly. Hazel eyes. I'm short. I'm a little…well, this gets tricky. I wouldn't say I'm fat, but I wouldn't say I'm thin. I'm a little more than average weight…I like my eye lashes. I like that um, I like, I've liked this for a long time, but like my leg hair is really light so if I don't shave, you can't really see it. I don't like my hands.

—Nicole

How would you describe the way that you look?
Short, chubby, chunky, brown hair, brown eyes. [She says this rhythmically, almost like a chant].

—Diana

There are two results of girls' objectification of their bodies. One, girls treat their bodies like distinct others, or two, they psychologically piece apart their bodies and work on them until their body becomes their accomplishment.

40

Both indicate an alienation of the self from body, although the first is most extreme.

A few girls treat their bodies like a whole separate entity, a friend, a character in their imagination. Girls' discussions about their bodies reveals this alienation of self and body. They construct narratives that clearly have two characters, the self and the body. They talk about their bodies as if they were not part of them but something or someone who was other than the self but with whom they were in relationship. For example, Danielle told me during our conversation about what she liked and did not about her body, "I'm tired of it [my body] being this big. I want to get it in shape. I'm gonna have to start taking it to the gym." Even more explicitly, Nicole talked about her body as another character at length.

> I do still always try to conform to a certain body image, but all of a sudden I realized that if I took what I had, and I like used them for what they were meant for, *then I could have so much more fun with my body, that I wouldn't have to fight with it, that I could get along with it, and we could play games together. You know what I mean, it didn't always have to be an issue and then we could have fun.* Like if I didn't try to scrunch myself into clothes that weren't designed for my body I wouldn't have to get upset about it not looking right in them, if I did find things that worked for me it didn't even become an issue.

41

Nicole talks about her body as a friend. It is a separate actor or character from her self. This alienation of body from self is not simply a result of psychic development in childhood but a defensive mechanism at adolescence that comes to solidify that childhood ability in some girls. These girls call upon their capacity to separate body and self and thus deflect the negative cultural judgments of their bodies from their selves. That is, separating body and self into two objects allows the criticism of one not to affect the other. Girls become very good at doing this.

Working-class girls get little recognition for their achievements, but they do get "compliments" on their appearances. It was clear simply from being at the working-class school that girls' appearances were a part of everyday discussions about girls. For example, I overheard a male guidance counselor and a male teacher discussing a female student whom they described as nice and as smart and then one of them added, "And she's one of the prettiest girls in the school." Similarly, above the din, in the rush of students between classes, one boy yelled to another about a girl who had just walked by, "She's one of those one's who's ugly and thinks she's pretty." Jen, like several other girls, told me that she and her mother "get along really well," but they argue about her appearance and her "fashion sense." When appearance becomes a key issue in a mother–daughter relationship, it takes on great importance.[93] Through these social contexts, girls learn that their appearances are something for which they will be recognized (either positively or negatively).

Thus, when I asked working–class girls about their goals and accomplishments, they often could not think of any, and would usually talk about their bodies. Working–class girls act on their bodies and make their bodies their "accomplishments" in an effort to reunite pleasure in their agency and their bodies. Acting on their bodies is also an effort to command some kind of recognition of their will from others. However, because they treat their bodies as separate from their selves and objectify their bodies, their efforts toward recognition and sexual subjectivity often fail. Working–class girls' objectifications of their bodies thus result in an alienated form of connection between agency and body.

Can you describe an important goal you achieved?
I love my hair. [She giggles.] My hair's my accomplishment 'cause I never thought I'd get it this long. Even though I think I'm a little bit chubby, I'm pretty happy with my weight because my family is known to be chubby. So keeping my weight down is difficult but I've done it.

—Jill

Is there a goal that you couldn't or had a hard time achieving?
Ummm. The only one would be like my physical weight. I'm always trying to maybe lose a little bit and firm up here and there and tone and I just don't have a lot of will power. That always gets a little frustrating 'cause I don't, I don't, I…I don't like my body weight, but that's what it does. Most of my goals that I set out to do I accomplished part of it at least. That's the only one I can think of.

—Esther

Have you ever set a goal and done something to achieve it?
Already achieved. Not fully, but I've gotten my complexion a lot cleaner than it was. I don't know. Maybe my hair or something. I don't know.

—Meghan

Working–class girls depict themselves as acting, deciding, and accomplishing with respect to this object—the body. It helps them to get or to feel like they can get some recognition for their agency. After they have made a bodily accomplishment, others comment on or "compliment" or recognize this accomplishment. For example, many girls answered the question, "What kind of things makes you feel good about yourself?" as Danielle did. "When someone like pays me a compliment on something, you know. Like says that I look nice or have on nice clothes or something."

However, girls sometimes set bodily or appearance "goals" that they cannot achieve, and this failure leaves them feeling badly about themselves. Weight, as discussed earlier, is a particularly good example of this. However, girls also get frustrated over hair, complexion, outfits, eye color, nose shape, and skin color. For example, I witnessed a minor example of this failure and its results when while on vacation visiting me, my thirteen-year-old cousin got her hair cut. The morning after the cut, when she had to style her hair by herself, she spent an hour trying to get it "right." When, in her view, she failed and could not fix it "right," her spirits and mood plummeted. She was frustrated both at not being able to *do* it and upset because she thought she would look "stupid" and "ugly" all day.

Women of color in particular are set up to fail if they try to meet normative beauty standards which hold up blonde blue-eyed women as the perfection of beauty. Chan found that Asian-American girls were less satisfied with their appearance than their non-Asian peers.[94] Also, Melissa, a middle-class Asian-American teen, told me, "Being Asian, people either think you are exotic or ugly, there's like nothing in between." All of girls' concerns over what appears to be shallow issues to many adults, are rooted in a desire to be a agentic, to accomplish something, and to receive recognition for one's accomplishment.[95]

43

SHAVING, THE EXCEPTION...

There is one pubertal event that does let girls experience some sexual subjectivity. This event is shaving. Because psychologists have done most of the research on puberty, the pubertal events previous research examines are biological. Social rites of passage like shaving, the one pubertal event boys and girls have in common, have not been studied.[96] Shaving legs and underarms is widely criticized by feminists who see it as ritual that shapes women into dolls, making them look plastic, like objects, or that makes women look like children who are hairless. For both genders, shaving *does* remove signs of bodily change, signs of gender and signs of adolescence and impending adulthood. However, shaving lets girls take pleasure in their agency and in their bodies. Their stories of shaving express a sense of "I did it" or even "I did it by myself." They feel like they have accomplished something independently. Jill talked more excitedly and more positively about shaving than anything else in the interview (except her boyfriend).

> The first time I found out about that was back with my cousin, Miranda, who is a month younger than I am. I slept over her house for the weekend. She said, "I'm gonna shave my legs." I was like, "I've never done

> that." And she was like "Come on, I'll show you." I can remember I cut
> myself, but my mother had never mentioned it, and this was just the
> coolest thing. *I just remember thinking this was the greatest thing, the coolest
> thing.* You know how you see it on tv or you hear older girls talking about
> it. I thought *"I'm so mature now."*

Similarly, Linda said, "I just did it. I just went ahead and did it. I asked my
mom, and *I just went ahead and did it on my own. I felt very grown up.*" Linda feels
like she did it herself, feels accomplishment, although she asked her mother's
permission to shave. Asking permission affords one recognition and confirmation (if permission is granted) of her new sense of being grown up.

Along with expressions of accomplishment, first shaving stories also have a
sense of "I like my body this way" and "My body makes me feel good." Girls
express these good feelings about their bodies after shaving by saying, "I felt
prettier, more feminine, skinnier, smoother." Or, "Honestly, I liked it 'cause it
made me look skinnier. I was smooth. I just remember thinking that." Kelly
told a more complicated story.

> I did it, and then I thought my mom would be mad, and so the whole
> point of shaving my legs was negated because I had to wear pants so she
> wouldn't find out. It was kind of neat I guess, I definitely felt like, petti-
> er or maybe more feminine or something, but I really couldn't show any-
> body 'cause I thought my mom would be mad. Finally, after I did it once
> or twice and the hair would grow back, I was going someplace, and I
> always wore stockings all the time, and I asked her if I could and she said
> yeah. And it was only after I asked her that I started nicking myself.

There is a sense that when they shave, girls feel good about at least part of
their bodies. Shaving is not as anxiety producing as other pubertal events. This
new aspect of their bodies—hair growth and its removal—does not make girls
as anxious about adulthood because shaving is not as associated with sexuality as menstruation and breast development are. Instead, shaving is associated
with femininity and identification with mother.[97] Fourteen-year-old Erin,
who was close to her mother, told me "I felt grown up. I was like, I can't
believe I did it! But I cut my leg and everything, it was just like…'Cause I
remember my mother, you know, when she had toilet paper on her legs when
she'd cut it, and I just felt like, I don't know, like I was her." For fifteen-year-
old Jen, shaving provided not only maternal identification, but ethnic identification as well. Her hairy legs that "needed" to be shaved confirmed that she
was like her mother, whom she described earlier in the interview as "full-
blooded Italian in every sense of the word," in gender and ethnicity.

When I was five I used to want to be like my mother, so I used to shave my legs until I cut off one of my fingernails, and that wasn't too good. I think my mother told me the right way to do it when it came time. I was eleven or twelve I think. I felt very grown up. Italians have nice hairy legs, you know, so I felt like my mother.

Two working-class girls did not achieve such a strong sense of bodily sub-jectivity when shaving. Both Kristen and Danielle did not correctly follow cultural prescriptions for shaving and were embarrassed by their mistakes.

I started shaving in third grade. My sister started shaving and she was in seventh grade and so like we start doing things at the same time. And ahhh, ah, I shaved my arms too! I thought if you have to shave your legs, you have to shave your arms too. So I shaved my arms and my legs and then my sister noticed I didn't have any hair on my arms, and I was like, "I shaved them." And, she was like "You idiot!" So that happened in third grade.

—Kristen

No one taught me. I did it on my own. (Pause.) And I did something so stupid! You're gonna die! I shaved my arms too! (Laughs and laughs.) I didn't know. I was just going out to a party, like a birthday party or some-thing, and I shaved my arms too! I can't believe I did that.

—Danielle

These girls did not feel as accomplished with their first shave because they felt they "did it wrong." Both recognized that part of the reason for their fail-ure was that they began shaving at a very young age. Many girls began shav-ing (as we also see above) well before puberty (some working-class girls in ele-mentary school) in an effort to imitate an older sister or their mother. Middle-class Cherri cut herself badly and therefore was also unable to achieve success in shaving, a sense of accomplishment, and a good feeling about her body because of shaving unsupervised at a young age.

Oh, I was in the bath tub, in my sister's bath tub, and I saw a razor, and umm, I was like wow, and I'd seen my sister use it, and I like worshiped her, and I wanted to copy her. So, I got out the soap, lathered up, and started shaving huge chunks of skin off, and then I started bleeding, 'cause you know, the first time you shave you don't know how to do it. I start-ed screaming and my mom thought I'd killed myself or something (laughs). So I ended up having to start shaving just 'cause I had these huge places with no hair on my legs. Anyway, so it was kind of on accident.

—Cherri

These three girls who did not take pleasure in their will and their bodies through shaving are the exception. For most girls shaving allows them to be more sexually subjective, although other pubertal events lead them away from sexual subjectivity and make them anxious about growing up and about their bodies.

BOYS...

Although we know much about the psychological development of identity in adolescent boys,[98] we know almost nothing about boys' experiences of puberty. Girls' pubertal events, especially menarche, have been more thoroughly researched than boys'. There has been minimal research on "spermarche," (first ejaculation) finding only that it is not a crisis or a negative experience for boys.[99] My data suggest pubertal events evoke cultural meanings about gender, bodies, and sexuality for boys as well as girls. Yet, I find that boys' experiences of puberty are less difficult than girls'. Boys tend to look forward to adulthood and seem less ambivalent about leaving childhood. It is not all unproblematic for all boys, but in general boys fare better than girls. I suggest that puberty is easier for boys because it becomes associated with adult masculinity, agency, and male sexuality which is culturally prized, not denigrated. These associations and experiences of puberty sustain self-worth. Boys learn through puberty that their bodies are active and able. The more adult their bodies, the more masculine, the better, since adult masculine bodies are culturally valued and admired.

Boys' experiences of puberty are less anxiety producing than girls' are. Boys express some uncertainty about their bodies throughout puberty, but they are better able to take pleasure in their abilities, their will, and their bodies much more often during puberty than girls are. Culturally, sexuality does not have as many negative associations for boys and men as it does for girls and women. With the exception of masturbation, sexuality for men is not associated with shame, dirt, danger, and taboo, but with adulthood, masculinity, and pride.

PUBERTAL SUBJECTIVITY...

In general, puberty facilitates the development of sexual subjectivity in boys. Changes in boys' bodies at puberty tend not to lessen boys' sense of agency and control, but further them. For example, when their voices change, boys do not experience their body as out of their control. When I asked Jack, a working-class eighteen-year-old, about his voice changing his answer was one I heard often. "I remember it, but it wasn't a big deal. I don't think it was that drastic either. I don't remember...I don't think it affects a lot of people. I don't think it's like a milestone." While some boys felt indifferent to their voice change, others often do something with their new voice. They "play with it" or they "save it," feeling it might have some valuable use. Still other boys say they use their new voice to make themselves appear older. Ted, a middle-class fifteen-year-old, claimed, "It wasn't a big deal to me. My brother hates it. I know that 'cause his is starting to right now. For me it was sort of funny. *I liked to play with it*, and whenever it broke I just sort of laughed." When I asked Brad about his voice changing and then if it embarrassed him, he seemed to think it was a ridiculous question.

It was about seventh grade, I remember it changed pretty early actually because, umm, all my teachers would say I was talking real loud, and I wouldn't notice it, and I told my mom, and she said, well, it's probably 'cause my voice is changing and sometimes I'd pick up the phone and people would think it was my dad for a second.
Were you embarrassed? How did you feel?
If anything I would've felt more grown up. When I went on vacation, I could pass for an older age or something. I thought that was kind of cool. Some people just thought I was older.

Boys use their changes of voice to do, to act. They are agentic with respect to this pubertal event, and they feel, more grown up. Boys also feel older and/or like their fathers when their voices change, and they talk about it with an underlying sense of pride as Brad does. Also, boys, like both Ted and Brad express keen interest in or amazement at their changing voice. They think it is "cool" or "fun." It seems a bit wondrous and interesting to them. They take pleasure in this bodily change.

The experience of shaving is similar for boys as for girls. It also provides boys with a feeling of accomplishment, a good feeling about their changing body, and an identification with their same sex parent. Boys take pleasure in shaving, even though they do not do all that much of it as teens. Listen to what Brent, Paul, and David said about shaving.

I tried it in seventh grade and I just shaved right here, sideburns, you know. Now I don't shave that much, maybe once a week or something. No one told me or helped me. *I did it just to feel kind of grown up*, to kind of pretend. Kind of an *ego booster* I guess.

—Brent

I was taught how to use an electric razor *by my father*. That was a while ago. It wasn't a big deal. It was just "yeah."

—Paul

47

I got a razor for my fifteenth birthday, which just passed. I lost it already but…I shave umm, I have to shave every few days and only on my side burns and *I like it. It makes me feel like my dad or whatever, like a grown up.*

—David

Both change of voice and shaving give boys pleasure in their will and pleasure in their changing bodies. Both pubertal events facilitate sexual subjectivity. However, unlike girls, boys are generally taught to shave by their fathers and figure out voice change on their own. Whereas many girls learned to shave from older sisters or friends (as well as mothers), or learned to use tampons from a best friend or older sister, pubertal changes for boys are less often discussed, learned, or experimented with among peers. First ejaculation, wet dreams, and masturbation (see below) are usually particularly isolating. Where girls are compelled by cultural norms to tell someone (usually their mother) about menarche, boys are expected to remain quiet about "spermarche." Thus, boys experience puberty in more isolation, and this may account for some of their expressions of uncertainty that accompany their descriptions of pubertal events that we will examine below.

The most negative feelings boys had about puberty were feelings of uncertainty. Puberty can be difficult for boys who lack cognitive knowledge about puberty. The knowledge that these boys felt most lacking is knowledge that confirms that they *are* now in puberty. Where girls often feel that their bodily changes are overly observed, some boys want more recognition of these changes and a confirmation of what they mean. Boys' pubertal changes are sometimes so subtle that boys are unsure of them when others do not comment on them. They wonder "Is my voice really changing? Do I really need to shave? Am I taller or do I just feel taller?" Doug "wondered" about pubic hair when it "started creating problems for me." These problems were hair getting caught in his underwear and clothes. He said he solved his problem by himself with "looser clothes." Some boys solved these problems of pubertal uncertainty with the help of parents and still others were never certain. Again, boys experience pubertal events in more isolation; that is they are less likely to talk at length about these events to parents, if it all, and they rarely discuss it with their peers.

My father taught me. I think I wanted to do it 'cause I had like spikes growing out and you didn't know if it was enough to shave or not to shave. I didn't think anything about it. It was not a big deal.

—Jack

It was, I think, freshmen year, and I was just like you know, wondering. I mean no one really killed [teased] me over "Your voice is changing." I was just like, is this like the *Brady Bunch*? Have you seen the one when Peter's voice changes? {*Yeah*} So I was like, oh is that it. I was like, should I save it or something? Should I talk? It wasn't that big a deal, but I was never really sure if that was it or if it was a sore throat.

—Eric

Eric's experience and reference to the *Brady Bunch* episode made me wonder whether another missing component of knowledge for boys is knowledge from media like television shows, books, and movies. Girls' pubertal events seem to be addressed more in this media. The exception may be masturbation. Male masturbation is a part of teen culture, jokes, teen movies where it is usually part of a joke or comedy, and more seriously in some juvenile novels for boys, like Judy Blume's *Then Again, Maybe I Won't.*

Masturbation still makes boys feel unsure of themselves. Although most adolescents now have access to information about masturbation through sex education classes, it is still the subject of many myths and fears. If boys have negative or anxious associations with sex at adolescence, they are about masturbation. However, Gaddis and Brooks-Gunn in examining experiences of first ejaculation in a small (eleven) sample of boys find that boys generally felt positively about first ejaculation.[100] That is, they felt excited, grown-up and happy and proud. Gaddis and Brooks-Gunn found little evidence of anxiety. However, first ejaculation is a one time event. Masturbation as a continued event may cause the somewhat greater anxieties I found here.

Before discussing boys' fears about masturbation further, let me say a word on girls. Masturbation also has negative associations for girls. No girls voluntarily mentioned it in the course of interviews, and the three working-class girls whom I tried to ask about it were embarrassed, silent, and said they did not masturbate. Their reactions caused me to stop asking about it because it made them so uncomfortable. Rosenbaum finds that many teenage girls think that masturbation is "something boys do," and they do not associate it with female sexuality.[101] Since, as we have seen, girls often say they do not like to touch or even to look at their genitals, it is not surprising that few teen girls, especially younger girls, masturbate. This issue does not disappear in adulthood. Laumann et al. found that adult women do not masturbate as much as adult men do. Where less than half of the women they surveyed had masturbated in the past year, more than six out of ten of the men had.[102]

Two middle-class fifteen-year-old boys voluntarily discussed masturbation without me asking them about it, and one boy said he was embarrassed by wet dreams until he saw his brothers' pornography that convinced him he was "not peeing in the bed." Their discussions, however, were retrospective. That is, they framed their comments with "When I was younger…" distancing themselves from embarrassment or other feelings of uneasiness. Their discussions were

49

about what they did not know or what they feared when they younger. Generally, they laughed at their younger selves. However, their comments reveal that younger boys do still worry that masturbation is somehow dangerous or wrong.

> I pretty much knew everything. I was only worried about getting AIDS through like masturbating or something (laughs), but umm, I actually talked to my dad about that so, I wasn't really worried about anything after sixth grade.
> *What did your dad say when you talked to him?*
> He said, he sort of laughed. He told me stories about how he used to do it too, and he said, "No, you can't get AIDS from doing that." And so I was happy, and he was happy, and that sort of opened the door for whatever conversations.
>
> —Brent

> I was a little worried about like masturbating and stuff at first. You know guys say things about it, and you're not sure [if they're true]. But once I got older, that stuff wasn't really of big concern. I didn't really care anymore.
>
> —Andy

50

These two boys suggest that boys' anxiety about masturbation subsides as they get older. Both of these boys turned to other men/boys, formally and informally, for information about masturbation and did so with differing results. One boy's father calmed his anxiety, where the latter boy's peers increased his. Masturbation is a topic among adolescent boys and between boys and men that seems to remain silent among girls and women.

Discussions of sex, serious or joking, facilitate bonds among men.[103] At puberty boys begin to develop more of these bonds, many of which are of a joking or boasting nature. Although at a deeper level they may be a way of expressing uncertainty and a fear of inadequacy, these jokes and boasts encourage feelings of adult masculinity in boys because they are a way of associating or bonding with adult men, and becoming adult men themselves. These bonds are quite different from girls' friendships in which aspects of sex and many issues about love are discussed sincerely, advisedly, and at length. Puberty is just the beginning of this joking relationship to sex and adult masculinity. It remains throughout adolescence and into adulthood.

OVERCOMING PUBERTAL UNCERTAINTY...

Despite the fears and uncertainties discussed above, boys come to associate pubertal change with adult masculinity, and they look forward to growing up.

Adult masculinity, as argued, is culturally different from adult femininity. It is valued and not negatively sexualized. Alone, this cultural idea of masculinity makes puberty easier for boys than for girls. However, parents and a good set of defenses also allow boys to move through puberty with more ease and emerge on the other side of puberty feeling positive, with their self-esteem intact.

First, parents, in particular, facilitate the association between pubertal change and adult masculinity. As boys get older, parents and others afford them more independence and more recognition of their selves, decisions, and accomplishments. When boys reach puberty, in general, they get taller; their bodies look more masculine; they begin to get facial hair; they grow physically larger. To parents, they look older, and thus, parents and others grant boys more independence and more recognition of their selves, decisions, and accomplishments. This is quite different from the ways that parents treat girls as they begin to look older. For girls, looking older means looking sexual and parents' response is toward greater restriction rather than greater independence. For example, I asked Doug, a middle-class seventeen-year-old, how he thought puberty had changed him or his life. He replied,

> [Before puberty] my parents would make me do things I didn't want to do and now they say "Okay, you're seventeen, you're old enough to decide for yourself." I guess They've given me more independence and less responsibility.

51

Brent, a middle-class fifteen-year-old, responded to the same question, "I've got more responsibilities and benefits. More freedom and that kind of thing, more relationships with girls." While puberty is not always easy for boys, they know that valued adult masculinity is on the other side of puberty. Girls see devalued, over-sexualized femininity on the other side of puberty.

Boys have several defenses that girls do not. Boys say that they look forward to moving beyond "childish" things. In fact, working-class boys, especially, distance themselves from any anxieties that puberty may cause by deeming them childish. I asked, Joe, a fifteen-year-old working-class boy, who was extremely confident in his intellectual ability, but less sure of his social skills, "Did your friends talk about puberty?" He replied, "Well, they're so childish they didn't really, no one would really talk serious, just fooling around and stuff. Like they say, like, how long your penis is and stuff like that." "Is it embarrassing?" I asked. "No," he said assuredly. Similarly, Paul, a working-class nineteen-year-old, couched his answer to whether boys worry about appearance and having muscles in terms of younger boys.

> I think [younger boys] worry about how they look. How they feel inside,
> it's like I'm not standing up to the rest of the guys. I mean that's what
> they're worried about, how they look, the superficial, and not who they
> are. It's really stupid and childish.

By calling anxieties about puberty "childish," many boys repress these anxieties
and construct a sense of self as an adult.[104]

Also, failure to live up to masculine standards of appearance does not feel
like personal failure to teenage boys, as failures to meet femininity standards
feel like shameful, personal failures to girls. Boys already have a defense at this
point in their development that girls do not. Boys are able to externalize negative feelings. When they do not live up to masculine standards of appearance,
boys simply tell a story where they blame their failures to achieve the ideal
masculine body type on something outside of themselves. They do not
attribute the flaws in the way they look to some failure in themselves and their
agency, as girls do. Middle-class boys, like Michael and Andy who are both fifteen, usually attribute their failure to have the ideal masculine body to a lack
of time. Michael, a sixteen-year-old middle-class boy, claimed, "I tried working out for a while, but then they changed the hours so I couldn't do it anymore, I didn't have time with school." Similarly, Andy said without apology, "I
did [work out] for a while, but then I just kind of let it go…Since I play a lot
of sports I get a pretty good workout. It's usually five days a week. So, that's
sort of my excuse, plus I don't have a lot of time." On the other hand, working-class boys usually attribute their lack of a perfect masculine body, especially "sufficient" muscle definition to money. Marc, a young boy (fourteen)
who had just barely reached puberty told me he would "like to have muscles
but we don't have enough money to buy weights, or so that I can go to a gym
or anything." Jim claimed his appearance in general, particularly the type of
clothes he wore, were the reason that he did not look the way he wanted to.
"We're not a very rich family, like other people can like afford better clothes
than me, and we just can't afford that. So I wish I could have better clothes
and stuff." Working-class boys more than any other group were aware of their
social class position, and here we see that they use that awareness to stave off
feelings of gender inadequacy. Thus, these boys in general told stories that
claimed "it is just my circumstance that is keeping me from being this ideal
version of masculinity, I'll get around to it when I have more time or money."
They do not feel a lack of subjectivity with respect to their appearances and
bodies.

Finally, we must acknowledge the silences in boys' stories. Culturally, boys
are allowed little leeway in discussing anxieties about bodies and sex, and perhaps this is why they present puberty as positively as they do. However, this
cultural prohibition may work as a defense for adolescent boys when they turn

it into repression of their anxieties about these issues. Boys' stories about puberty and self were far more seamless, smooth, and uncontradictory than girls' were. Whether they had "forgotten" the complications of puberty or simply refused to talk about them, this defense seemed to be working because their descriptions of their selves were, generally, positive and agentic.

BOYS, BODIES, AND SELVES...

Thus, as teenagers just beyond puberty, the boys in my sample described their bodies and selves in generally positive ways, especially compared with girls' descriptions. Ted described his appearance, "I'm tall I guess. I'm happy with everything about my body, except for my acne." Jim said, "Kind of average height. A little bit overweight, ah you know. I don't really judge myself a lot. I think I'm kind of mediocre in the face. I can tell like if a boy is really, if a girl is gonna like him or if she's gonna puke, but I think I'm all right." John, a working-class sixteen-year-old, summed up his appearance by pointing to his ethnicity. "I have dark hair. I have brown eyes. I look Asian, 'cause I am." John may have found that in going to a primarily white school, saying one was Asian was all that was needed to describe his appearance, since it was different from most of his peers. Several girls also added ethnicity to their descriptions of themselves, but their descriptions were still much more detailed than these boys. For example, Nicole said, "I'm really short, I have dark curly hair, green eyes, and I look Jewish and Polish, and I'm kind of stocky and, I'm really forward, 'cause it even comes out in the way I look, I just look forward, and I know that."

53

Boys had little problem telling me about their whole selves as girls often did. For example, Eric, a middle-class seventeen-year-old, said in detail that he was intelligent, proud, and independent.

> I guess I'm intelligent. I like challenges, and I like puzzles a lot. Umm, I guess I'm not too good working in groups. I like better having like a few close friends than a group of friends. Umm, I love games and anything intellectually challenging...I've resisted the urge to conform so I feel pretty proud of myself when I do that or else when I like, like last year in biology we were doing genetics and I found this way that for me seemed so much simpler than you know, you have to draw those squares, and just a way of multiplying ratios and when I explained it to the teacher that's the way that geneticists do and I figured it out by myself!

However, where girls had a difficult time describing their selves, boys had a difficult time describing how they looked. Their descriptions of their appearances were much briefer than girls' descriptions. Many of my conversations with boys about their appearances were much shorter than those with girls and more confusing. These conversations often went like this:

How would you describe the way that you look?
How I look? I don't know. Kind of average I guess.
—working-class fifteen-year-old boy.

Can you describe how you look?
I…what do you mean like?
If someone didn't know you, or couldn't see you, how would you describe your appearance?
Oh, umm, I'm short I guess. Brown hair. Brown eyes.
—middle-class fifteen-year-old boy.

Boys may find this question of describing their appearance difficult and may be vague because they are less worried about it or because they have such an integrated sense of self and body that they cannot extract simply physical descriptions of themselves. Further evidence of body and self integration appears when boys talk about playing sports or lifting weights. Unlike girls, who claim that their bodies and appearance affect how they feel about themselves, boys claim that how they feel about themselves affects how they look. Brent, who "works out" a lot said explicitly, "I think the way I look is affected by how I feel. I'm bound to be more attractive when I'm more confident, definitely." Boys' discussions also indicate that they have a sense of acting in their bodies. For example, Jack described this very seriously,

I don't know if it's important to have muscles, but mentally I feel better. I've been working out again now for two weeks and I feel better. You just feel better the way you hold yourself. I think it's more of a mental thing than it is for a physical look at yourself in the mirror—well actually that's part of it too, you look better, or you feel like you look better whether you actually do or not. Or whether it's just mental perception of how you look.

Thus, Jack suggests that if he is physically active, "works out," then he feels better about himself, not because his actual body has changed but because of the experience, the doing of "working out."

Similarly, David, who is fifteen and middle-class, says that playing sports makes him feel better psychologically and makes him feel agentic, like he has "accomplished something." Notice that this accomplishment is something he did through using his body, not through acting on his body, as girls do. Using his body makes him feel good about himself. When I asked if he played any sports he replied,

> I ski. I sort of play basketball. I started volleyball for the first time this year. I really liked it. I really like sports, athletics. It kind of helps me out, to reduce stress and that kind of thing. I really work hard at that. I feel tired and good, like I've really accomplished something.

Few girls discussed sports this way, although sports did seem to encourage a more positive sense of body and self in girls who were athletes. (See Chapter Six for further discussion of this issue.)

Ryan, a working-class sixteen-year-old, specifically discussed being in and feeling comfortable in his body when playing sports. He said, "Soccer is my favorite. It's just a real physical sport. It's a lot of, it's probably one I work the hardest at. I feel comfortable playing. I don't feel awkward doing it. I have a good body for it." He connects using his body to feeling "in" his body. I suggest that this sense of acting in one's body is a sign of sexual subjectivity. These boys suggest that they take pleasure in their agency and their bodies simultaneously. They feel like they accomplish things in their bodies and in their lives.

Some boys came right out and said that they were agentic accomplishers. They spoke with such an air of confidence, I got the sense that they truly believed that nothing could hold them back. This was particularly the case with Paul, a working-class nineteen-year-old athlete.

55

> *Tell me about yourself.*
> I'd say I'm outgoing. I set out to do things and I accomplish them. And, I have a set of goals, and I want to achieve those goals.
> *What kind of goals?*
> Goals in life. Like if I want to do something and do it good, then I'll eventually do it.

During the course of being interviewed, boys also presented selves that were very different from those that girls presented. After interviewing the first five girls in my study, I interviewed the first boy and wrote in my field notes, "There *is* a difference between girls and boys. Before this interview I thought I wouldn't find a difference between girls and boys. But, this boy was calm, assured, and he's younger than the girls I've already interviewed. He answered every question immediately without hesitation. He wasn't tentative in his language. The girls all "um"-ed and "like"-d and changed their minds, never wanting to quite commit. He also sort of challenged me on not wanting to answer one of the questions. His whole demeanor was just so different…" As

it turned out, not all boys were this confident, but boys were much more likely to present this type of self than girls were.

There are, of course, exceptions. Puberty is not easy for all boys. In particular, the only literature on puberty that compares boys and girls finds that
although being an early developer makes the experience more negative for
girls, being a late developer is more negative for boys.[105] Being a late developer is more negative for boys because boys gain status as they begin to look
older and bigger. Boys who remain small and continue to look childlike well
into their teens are more likely to be teased about their size and strength by
peers. However, the literature that finds that being late for boys is negative is
not conclusive. Petersen and Crockett find improved well-being in late developing girls *and* boys.[106] This may be because some late developing boys find
ways to compensate for size and strength. For example, Thorne says many
small boys in the elementary schools where she did ethnography were picked
on because of their size, but then she describes Kevin who "was also short, but
he did not receive these ritual reminders [hair tousling, being pinned from
behind, that other small boys did], perhaps because he was unusually skilled in
athletics and a member of the group of boys with the highest status."[107]

Similarly, two working-class boys in my sample who appeared to be late
developers had very different experiences. Jim, who served mass in his community's Catholic church, boasted that he was a "genius" in math and was
involved in many school activities like student council. However, he was generally nervous throughout the interview, thought the popular kids were "stupid," and said that sometimes "you get teased about sports and stuff, but it's just
childish. It doesn't really bother anyone." He generally did not seem to be
happy and led me to believe he was not a "popular" kid, but was the walking
the line between "normal" and "geek." Adam, however, who was also small and
apparently a late developer, approached the interview with an air of confidence. He played hockey and soccer and played them well, as he "started" on
both teams. Among these working-class kids, athletic talent was highly prized
for boys and brought much status. Thus, Adam's experience of puberty and
sense of self were both more positive than Jim's even though they both were
late developers. Perhaps if Jim had gone to one of the private schools where I
also interviewed, he too would have been able to overcome the low status of
being a late developer because of his talent in math. In these schools, "being
smart" was valued in a way it was not in the working-class public school. There
"being smart," especially if that was all one was (without athletic skill or other
markers of status), was equated with "being a geek." Thus, in these ways class,
talent and skill, and physical development all combine to create particular
hierarchies that shape late developing boys' experiences of puberty.

Puberty and adolescence are also difficult for boys who do not conform to
normative standards of masculinity. This was particularly true at the working-

class public school. Appearance, manner, and dress for working-class boys was much more narrowly defined than it was among the middle-class boys. Most working-class boys wore jeans and t-shirts or sweatshirts, denim jackets, and high-top sneakers. Some of the "jocks" wore hockey shirts or football shirts. The "burnouts" or "stoners" often wore concert t-shirts.[108] Their hair was cut short and unstyled or was shoulder length and shaggy. One day while I was waiting in front of the school, there were two boys standing around also waiting for a ride. A third boy, who looked very different from the other two and from most of the other boys at this school, walked out of the school and down the hill. This boy had on clothes that were "fashionable"—a vest, polished leather shoes instead of sneakers, a bright colored shirt with a collar, a gold hoop earring (or two)—and a styled hair cut. One of the boys who was waiting for a ride said to the other, "He's a boy, but his parents brought him up to be a girl. He's got all the parts I do. He's a boy! But, his parents made him a girl." This was an insult to this boy's gender identity and masculinity. They did not explicitly suggest that this boy was gay which would be the worst possible insult among the (homophobic) boys at this school. Regardless, it was clear that those who did not conform to this school's normative masculinity would suffer insult, teasing, and rumor. Much research confirms that feminine and/or gay boys and men often receive this treatment.[109]

Adolescence denotes "the psychological processes of adaptation to the condition of pubescence."[110] In other words, adolescence is a time for making sense and self out of a newly changed body. Despite the importance placed on puberty in such an understanding of adolescence, there has been little empirical research on the gendered effects of puberty on adolescents' selves. What there is, is not theoretically driven,[111] and most studies are quantitative.[112] We know a lot about attitudes, behavior, knowledge, values, and some about positive and negative affect, but little about the emotions, meanings, and feelings that puberty evokes. Most studies of puberty, like the studies of early and late developers,[113] investigate puberty in terms of "more or less" puberty. That is, which adolescents are better off if they are further along in pubertal development (boys) and which are better off if they have not developed as much (girls)? All this research has reduced adolescents' emotions to positive or negative affect or indifference.[114] This research does not address the quality of the positive or negative emotions. Are these positive emotions joy, relief, or satisfaction? Are these negative emotions shame, anger or fear? Except for the research on early versus late developers, most of the literature on the social/psychological experiences of puberty does not compare girls and boys.

However, as we have seen there are significant differences in the ways that boys and girls experience puberty. In particular, adolescent boys and girls feel very differently about their bodies and thus their selves as they develop through puberty and emerge into mid-adolescence. Girls' feelings of shame, objectification, and fear that are created by menstruation and breast development more negatively affect their self-worth than boys' feelings of pubertal uncertainty affect theirs. These very different constructions of self are then brought to dating, romantic relationships, and first sexual experiences, as we see in the following chapter.

"I COULDN'T EVER PICTURE MYSELF HAVING SEX..."

Gender Differences in Sex and Sexual Subjectivity

*I think there are very few girls I know who are having
sex and actually enjoying it, most say it hurts especially the first time. The guys who are being promiscuous
are actually enjoying it.*

      —middle-class seventeen-year-old girl.

chapter 4

WHY DO adolescents have sex? What kinds of internal and external factors
influence their decisions to have sex? Is the experience of teenage sex different for boys and girls? These questions are left unanswered by much of the
current research on teen sex. Chilman in describing teen sex research says
that, "In general, many of the studies seem to be voyeuristic. Who does what,
sexually, with whom, how, and when?"[115] She is right. Researchers have
extensively studied the demographics of teenage sex[116] and sexual knowledge, attitudes, and behaviors.[117] Yet, there is little research about the experience of sex—if teens like it or not, how it makes them feel about themselves,
if girls feel differently about it than boys do. "What sexuality means to adolescents, how it relates to other aspects of teenage life, and what strategies
teens use to manage or incorporate it into their lives have not been studied

in detail."[118] This chapter begins to fill this gap, again paying close attention to gender differences in agency and sexual subjectivity.

Throughout this chapter when I talk about "sex" I mean sexual intercourse because this is what teenagers mean when they talk about sex. There is a socially constructed line between all other forms of sexual petting and intercourse in teen culture. Intercourse is invested with more meaning and significance than any other act. I find that like puberty, first sexual experiences further solidify agency and sexual subjectivity in boys. Girls, however, feel less agentic and less sexually subjective after first sexual experiences.

In order to examine how teens further construct sexual subjectivity (or not), we need to understand why and how teens come to have sex, for the gender differences in the social and psychodynamic paths to first intercourse are telling. By paths to sex, I mean teens interactions around, feelings about, expectations and knowledge about sex that cause teens to have sex. These include the meaning of dating or "going out" or having a boyfriend or girlfriend, expectations and experiences of sex, and the immediate social interaction between two teens, the "talk" or lack of it, that leads to sex.

IDEAL LOVE...

Dating, "seeing each other" (dating) and "going out" (having a long term monogamous relationship, the step after "seeing each other")[119] are all important cross gender relationships that organize teen social life. For the most part, these relations mimic those of teens' images of adulthood. In them, most teens practice traditional gender roles and heterosexuality. This is true for both class groups and both genders. But these relationships do not only mimic adult heterosexuality, they also mimic children's play. Thorne and Luria observe that kids often play games that are "girls against the boys."[120] This oppositional gender strategy is carried into early stories of romantic relationship. Whenever boys complained about girlfriends or girls about unfaithful boyfriends, their stories took on this tone of the girls against the boys. For example, the boys whom I interviewed complained about their girlfriends, commitment, and monogamy.[121] They said things like nineteen-year-old Paul did, "I'm trying not to attach myself right now, until I go away to school. I don't want to deal with anyone in high school. I don't want to carry any baggage." Boys freely admitted that one was not supposed to admit to liking his girlfriend in teenage boy culture. I asked Scott, a working-class eighteen-year-old, "Do guys talk about their girlfriends?"

> I don't ever talk to my guy friends about my girlfriend, except...well you never admit that you like her, never. You just say that she was a pain in the neck.

Girls, on the other hand, are immersed in romantic culture. They told stories of love…

> *Tell me about your boyfriend.*
> I love his personality. The way he treats me. The way he says he cares for me, it's really important to me. He's very outgoing. Umm, he's real funny, and he makes me laugh. Umm, he's, I think he's real nice lookin'. And he's not too tall. He's about 5'8". So, he's just perfect.
>
> —Valerie

…and sometimes of unfaithful boyfriends who betrayed them.

> He's really stubborn, and he didn't care about anything, and he lied, he lied all the time. He wasn't loyal at all or anything like that.
>
> —Diana

Psychoanalytic authors suggest that many girls and adult women take up a position of ideal love in relationship to their fathers in order to get vicarious access to subjectivity. Ideal love is submission to and adoration of an idealized other whom one would like to be like and from whom one wants confirmation and recognition. It is a form of identificatory love. Ideal love explains, according to Benjamin, why women's love often takes the form of the worship of a hero that a woman would actually like to be herself.[122]

61

At adolescence, many girls, in the process of growing up and away from their families, shift their ideal love from their fathers to male peers. The project of ideal love and the shift of ideal love from fathers to male peers is simultaneously a social and a psychodynamic one. By shifting their ideal love to male peers instead of fathers, girls can be recognized as participating in the adult world of heterosexual romance. Adolescents usually want to be recognized as grown up, independent, and able to do things. I argue that many girls, especially working-class girls, find ideal love to be the only route (although often an alienated one) to attaining agency and sexual subjectivity, and it has a particularly strong force in girls' heterosexual relationships at this age.

Teen culture emphasizes compulsory heterosexuality and facilitates girls' move to ideal love with male peers. There are very few lesbian or gay teen romance novels and thousands of heterosexual ones. Television shows that are geared to teens, like *Beverly Hills 90210*, and soap operas, a favorite past-time of many teens, rarely have gay characters and never have regular gay characters. However, heterosexuality and the adventures it poses almost entirely comprise the plots of such shows. There is little room for gay or lesbian identity or desire in most of this adolescent pop culture. This may be part of the reason why establishing a gay or lesbian identity as a teen is a difficult and relatively new phenomenon, as well as why many gay and lesbian teens also have had heterosexual experience.[123] This emphasis on compulsory heterosexuality shapes all girls' and boys' (although boys are less caught up in romantic culture) fantasies and realities.

In early adolescence, girls, especially white working-class girls, become absorbed in teen idols, teen romances, and pop rock ballads about love.[124] Then, as teens, many girls acquire boyfriends and construct narratives about their boyfriends that cast them in the light of ideal love. Stories of ideal love are not stories of passion and sexuality but are stories of romance and what sociologist Arlie Hochschild calls magnified moments. A magnified moment is "a moment of heightened importance to the individual. This can be an epiphany, a moment of intense glee, or unusual insight. Within cautionary stories, it can be a moment of unusual despair."[125] First dates, first looks, first meetings, as well as break ups, all are or contain magnified moments for girls in ideal love.

In narratives of ideal love girls often describe boys as heroes. They are "heroes of the high school"—athletes, military men, reggae singers, exceptional artists, boys who speak foreign languages, and older boys. Which boys are considered heroes depends on class. A smart boy is probably a "geek" at the working-class high school, but a potential hero and ideal love at the private, middle-class high school. Girls also sometimes compare boys to their fathers, providing the connection to early childhood rapprochement and first ideal love that Benjamin proposes.

The best way to understand what ideal love is, is to hear girls describe it to you. They get excited, interested. Their stories become detailed, and these details, however insignificant and minor they may be to the listener, are clearly important to the narrator. Their stories also get infused with romantic language and romantic words—flowers, fairy tale, letters, swept off my feet, magic, flirting, intense, beach, cute, beautiful, secrets. Descriptions of ideal love also clearly have a story to them. The narrator has put the events together to make a "fairy tale sort of story" for herself. I asked Jill to tell me about her boyfriend (a question that was always met with enthusiasm and to which I always got a long answer).

> It's a fairy tale sort of a story. He's in the Marine Corps, and he was over in the Middle East during the war. And there were names in the newspaper you could write to, and I wrote to a Sergeant, and he'd just gotten married and felt really awkward writing, so he gave the letter to my boyfriend, Alan. Alan and I wrote and when he came back to the States he sent me flowers and asked if he could meet me, and once he came up to meet me we've been together ever since. That's last year. He's stationed in the south. I just came back from visitin' him. It's really far. He's getting

out the end of May; so we won't have to do that any more. Anyway, he's wonderful. He's a spitting image, like inside, how he acts, of my dad. My father always said, like teasing me when I was little, wait, you'll find someone exactly like me. And it's true. He's quiet. He only speaks his mind when asked. He's very secretive about his feelings. I've just started tapping into them myself. He'll do anything to help anyone out. Our relationship is going well. We communicate really good. He can mumble on about something for five minutes and someone else would be truly lost but I'd know exactly what he's talking about. We really trust each other, and I don't trust really easily and he doesn't either. He's had a bad past, and I have a bad past, so…

Kristen, told a less complicated version of ideal love, and like Jill's military man, her ideal love is not an ordinary guy, but a reggae singer. He has special status. She told me about him at the beginning of our interview when I asked her what she daydreamed about.

> I always think about this guy I met this summer. I wicked fell in love, wicked bad. I didn't just love him, but I wicked fell-in-love. You know, swept me off my feet. I just think about his face, the way he used to sing to me. He was wicked awesome. He used to like sing reggae to me. He was awesome. He was just one of a kind.

63

Even ex-boyfriends can be ideal loves. Stories of ex-ideal loves are similar to those of current ideal loves, except the ending to the story is different. Somewhere in the story there is usually a fatal flaw discovered or an unanticipated event, a magnified moment, that leads to the breakup. The tone of these stories shifts from romantic, to sad, to angry.

> *Tell me about him [your ex-boyfriend].*
> Well, he was intelligent. I mean, I don't look for intelligence as a primary factor anymore. I like going out with guys and I like being with them, but there are so many, in high school at least, either they are stupid or they act that way 'cause they think it's cool. But he was really intelligent. He, we can really talk. I mean, it wasn't just talk about like other people or like whatever, since we live so far away. We talked about like real things. We had like these really intense phone conversations until like one o'clock in the morning. I mean it was of course like difficult because in Europe [where they met], we did not do anything like romantic or kiss or anything at all, and then it was all like through the phone, and we started out, just like, kinda flirting. And then it just kind of got worse and worse and then it was just kind of like more and more and more intense

you know. Everybody like almost saying what they mean, almost, almost, almost. And then one day, he just like wrote me this letter. "I think you're so beautiful inside and out, and I can't believe you know, that I didn't take advantage of the chance to get to know you better in Europe but…" You know, he ended the letter, like, "I think I love you." And I was like "OH MY GOD!" 'Cause I had been in love with him for like, I mean, well not like a long time, but for like three weeks. I really just knew. It was really wonderful. It was a great feeling, like a secure feeling. And that's one of the reasons that it really pissed me off that it didn't work out after a while. I was like "This is a big deal, this is right you know. We're in love why isn't everything perfect?" I'm kinda like mad at him right now. I've called and I've written him letters but he just doesn't return any of it. And I had a lot of higher hopes for him at least, 'cause we were so close.

—Juliana

First meetings with ideal loves are often magnified moments. Danielle described one of the most magnified moments I heard in all my interviews. Her first meeting with her boyfriend was a magnified moment in itself, yet within this general story, there was literally one specific moment that she magnified—when she and the boy turned to each other and said the exact same thing at the same time. It was clear to me as the listener that this was the moment that cinched the story that they were "right" for each other because she prefaced the moment in her telling with a breathless, giggling "I have to tell you this."

How did you meet your boyfriend?
We met in August of last year. We met on the beach! It was real cute. Me and my friends were walking down the beach and three guys kept driving by in this car, and they're always like, "Hey, State College" 'cause I had this State College shirt on. And umm, they're like "Do you want a ride?" They looked nice. They weren't dirty or anything. So I'm like "Sure!" Well, I waited for my friends to decide. And we got in and we hung out at the beach. And like he chased after me 'cause they were trying to pull us in the water. It was sooo fun! I'll never forget it. And then like…I have to tell you this! He chased after me, and like he grabbed me and started swinging me around and I'm like "Aaaah!" and I got a big mouth. He's going "Promise you're not gonna scream. Promise you're not gonna scream if I let you go. Come on, shhh. They're gonna think I'm raping you or something." So he let me go and then we're walking back to where my friends are and then we both look at each other and go "You run too fast." And it was so cute! Then that night he called me at

like twelve o'clock and we talked 'til like five in the morning. And a couple of weeks later we started going out.

Over half of all the working-class girls in my sample told stories of ideal love as compared to one quarter of the middle-class girls. One reason for this is that working-class girls, who get little acknowledgement of their agency in other spheres, get recognition from others when they "accomplish" the task of acquiring a boyfriend. When I asked Linda, "What things make you feel good about yourself?" she replied, "When a guy calls me and asks me out on a date! Ahhh! That's the best. My mom can't believe I have so many dates." Esther, a working-class girl, said that she clearly got that message that boys, and especially a husband, were important accomplishments. They were things (among several others) that she and her mother fought about a lot.

> The most recent thing is I'm moving in with my boyfriend, and that's out of wedlock. She's a strict Catholic and that's a big thing, she wants me to get married ASAP, and she's bitching for more grandchildren, too. So she's really pushing that on me. We fight about my clothes, the way I act, how she doesn't like my way of reasoning or thinking. She thinks I'm too, I don't know, liberal, I guess maybe is the word. She thinks I'm just too outgoing for my own good. So she's always telling me about that, but the big thing is marriage right now.
> *So you don't want to get married.*
> No. No. I haven't even graduated from high school, and my big thing right now is just trying to start college.

Mothers, however, are not the only ones who think boyfriends are important for girls. Peers also see having a boyfriend as a sign of status and of accomplishment. Kendra claimed, "It's so important to have a boyfriend because it's really a sign...to have something saying you're really attractive to someone is really important."

Another reason for this class difference in ideal love, is, as we will see in Chapter Five, middle-class girls remain in ideal love with their fathers well into adolescence in contrast to working-class girls who switch their allegiance quite early. Middle-class girls' ideal love of their fathers not only facilitates their feelings of agency but delays their sexual involvement with boyfriends. For, as we will see below, girls often have sex in order not to lose their ideal love.

The propensity toward ideal love in these working-class teenage girls does offer them one source of agency. Because of ideal love, working-class girls are more likely to break through the "tyranny of nice and kind" that Brown and Gilligan describe. Several working-class girls made it clear that they were not subjected to Brown and Gilligan's "tyranny of nice and kind." This group of working-class girls often said that they "had to" speak their mind or that they were "loud." Usually they were mean and unkind when fighting about boys or defending their own reputations with boys. For example, Amanda, a savvy fifteen-year-old who talked at length about her boyfriends and the "guys" she met at the mall, described how she stuck up for herself in a fight with another girl who thought Amanda was stealing her boyfriend, which Amanda was.

> Like the other night she called me and I was just so mad. I was like, "I'm just fucking friends with him!" And I was yelling 'cause I have a big mouth and then she said something, something...I can't remember but something "cunt" and then she was like, "I'm gonna nail you." And I was like, I'd kill her. She's so stupid, I could kill her. But like I wouldn't touch her unless she touched me first [points to her chest].

Thompson explains that there is a connection between this fighting and ideal love in working-class girls' lives.

> What girlfighters fight for, and those who fear girls fall back on, is dyadic intimacy: the one boy or man on whom they lay all the chips of life. In the empathy of first love, they get this from the boys they will fight to keep forever. This is their great hope—the achievement that will make up for everything else: for being raised to serve men, for being their mothers' daughters.[126]

Thompson finds, as I do, that boyfriends are so important because a life organized around a man and mothering is many poor and working-class girls' only vision of the future.

But what about boys' roles in teenage love relationships? Boys do not usually reciprocate or lend support to girls' stories of ideal love. Take for example the boyfriend and girlfriend who told me how they met. The girl's story was full of the language of magnified moments and ideal love. The boy's story was very straight forward. He told me "I think we met at the pool." She told me a much longer story. She said that they met at a party on Valentine's Day right after she had broken up with her last boyfriend. She had not wanted to go to the party, but her friends talked her into it. He had spent all night talking to her and teasing her, and then the next day he and his friends came in to where she worked. She was embarrassed because she charged him the wrong amount for something he bought, and she worried he would not like her anymore. She added at the end of her story that she had told him that he would never forget their anniversary, since it was Valentine's Day. Apparently, he had forgotten, or had not wanted to subscribe to such a romantic version of how they had met.

Boys rarely used the word love in discussing their feelings about their girlfriends or relationships. Love was something that they expressed to girls only reciprocally or out of awkwardness. Brent's story best exemplifies this phenomenon.

> I didn't think anything was going to happen between us, but she was spending the night at my house, well, she stayed in my room, so I was just like on the bed, and she was on the floor and she was telling me about everything that was going on. And like I went down to hug her and everything, and she wouldn't let go and so I don't know how long we were hugging or anything, but we started kissing and it...God it was so strange and she told me that she loved me in the middle of it all, and (laughs) I knew a little bit more about what it meant than I did in sixth grade, what was I gonna say "Oh thanks?" So I told her I loved her too, but I knew I didn't really, umm, I mean...

Boys seem to be looking for a blend of friendship and sex in relationships with their girlfriends. They are not looking for romance or ideal love. Empirical research finds that men's friendships (and I suspect this is also true of teen boys' friendships) are based on doing things together rather than on talking or sharing emotions (as women's friendships are).[127] Talking, or having a "close" friend, is what some boys get and are looking for in relationships with their girlfriends. However, even boys who admit to wanting friendship, comment on the burden of commitment. Joe told me that he "went out with this girl for like a year, and I liked her a lot. We talked and went a lot of places together." Notice how brief his description of his girlfriend and their relationship is compared to girls' descriptions of their boyfriends. Since Joe did not seem very enthusiastic about his previous girlfriend I asked him, "Would you want to have a girlfriend now?" He replied, "Yeah, someone to talk to a lot. Like a good friend. Well, you also get too serious and get tied down a lot." I received this answer from many boys. They emphasized wanting a girlfriend, to have a friend, but not wanting too much commitment.

> *Would you want to have a girlfriend?*
> Yeah, well, I don't really have any real close friends, I have a lot of friends, but not really close, there's no one like close friend. The disadvantages would be that it's a lot of commitment, I think.
>
> —Rick

Would you want to have a girlfriend?

It'd be someone to be with and talk to, but I feel that I wouldn't like, like, to feel that I have to devote a certain amount of time every night calling them.

—Eric

Given the short length of most teen relationships, boys' fears of and complaints about commitment seem unwarranted (or perhaps their fears of commitments are what cause such short relationships). I suspect that complaining about commitment and the amount of time one has to spend with a girlfriend has become part of establishing a sense of adult heterosexual masculinity. Finally, boys rarely express the feelings of romantic love that girls do. In particular, their stories have little of the romance, sadness, or melodrama that girls' stories have. There is little in boys' stories that suggest they are playing out a romantic narrative. Also, boys' stories, especially when they become stories of breaking up, often contain hostile feelings. I asked Paul why he started "going out" with his girlfriend.

I think I liked her innocence. At first it was great. We could laugh and everything, but then we started to fight. I was like "forget it."

Why did you break up?

Well, put it this way. She has a wicked attitude, like and I was stupid. I ended it and she changed her attitude. Fine. I thought I'd give her a second chance this year, turned out she had the attitude again so I said goodbye.

What kind of attitude did she have?

Well, "I can't change" or "This is me, I'm sorry I can't be nicer." It's like, no! She still has the attitude. She has a mouth that I'd like to stick a bar of soap in for two hours. So I don't want to deal with that.

This story is very different from those we hear from girls, even girls who have broken up with their boyfriends. Finally, we will see below that sex, too, is less tied to love (as the old story goes) for boys than for girls.

EXPECTATIONS AND EXPERIENCES OF SEX...

Teenaged girls and boys have very different expectations and experiences of sex. Girls' expectations of sex range from romantic images portrayed by the media to fears that it will hurt, be painful, or scary, with the majority (well over half) falling in the latter category. There are no class differences or differences based on whether or not the girl had sex. I asked Tiffany about her first experience of sex, "Was it what you expected it to be like?" "No. Not at all. I expected the movie type thing." Erin had not yet had sex and thought,

I think that when you love somebody a real lot, I think that it's gonna be great, and umm, just like everything that's going on like with AIDS and pregnancy. It's scary. So once you're like using birth control and you check for AIDS and things like that, other STD's, and you're not worried at all, then it's just like the only thing you're gonna be thinking about is that other person, and it's gonna be good, but if you're distracted by all those other things, I think it's gonna take away from it.

Kristen had similar reservations,

I'm pretty scared 'cause of all the stories I've heard. And with STD's now I mean it's really scary. You can't be sure who he's been with. I mean they may say "I've only been with one other girl before and I was only with her once" or whatever and you don't know that. Umm, also, like doing the right thing. 'Cause you hear so many stories but like if it really comes down to it would I perform right or whatever? They say the first time hurts a lot, I don't know.

Other girls' expectations were even more negative. Amy, like many girls, said, "I thought it was gonna hurt really, really bad…" And, Jill thought sex was "gross" when she was younger.

I thought it was disgusting! Until eighth grade. And I was appalled, and I thought it was the grossest thing. Umm, hearing friends talk about it, I did have friends who had sexual intercourse in the middle school, and they would tell everyone about it or whatever and I thought it was like disgusting!

Boys, on the other hand, had generally positive expectations about sex. They thought it would be pleasurable, and many said they looked forward to it or were curious about it. However, because boys are culturally supposed to think sex is good, it may have been more difficult for them to express negative expectations, although not impossible. Middle-class boys were able to express some of their anxieties about sex. They claimed a few more anxieties and were slightly less positive about their expectations than working-class boys who were more invested in maintaining normative masculinity. Middle-class boys described expectations like Greg, a middle-class sixteen-year-old, and Dennis.

I expect it to be good. I hope it's good. I know guys who have done it and just really regretted it afterwards.

—Greg

> I look forward to it. It's an experience I haven't had and I wonder what it's like, and I'll also be real nervous about how she feels and what it would be like and if I'd do it right, just basically that.
>
> —Dennis

Dennis' admission that he worried whether or not he would "do it right" may be the most prevalent worry that boys have about sex. Laumann et al. found that young men (age 18–24) were most likely to have "anxiety about performance."[128]

Working-class boys, like Adam, Scott, and Rick, however, said they had few expectations about sex at all or only positive ones. They claimed respectively, "I'll just wait for the time to come. I'm not gonna worry about it"; "I thought it would be great. I couldn't wait to do it"; and "I think it'll be all right. I don't think it'll be scary or anything."

These expectations are in sharp contrast to girls'. No girl said that she looked forward to sex or that she expected it to be pleasurable.[129] Girls also have sex later than boys do, although girls more or less catch up in their late teens. In my sample about half of the girls (seventeen) and boys (ten) had had sex. However, according to Hayes, at age fifteen only 5% of girls and 17% of boys have had sexual intercourse.[130] The percentage of both groups of teens who are sexually active increases as teens get older. By age eighteen 44% of girls and 64% of boys have had sexual intercourse. By age twenty most unmarried men and women are sexually active; over 80% of men and 70% of women have had sex once. (African-American teens and teens from lower socioeconomic class backgrounds have sex earlier than whites and those from higher socioeconomic class backgrounds.) This gender difference in age may be attributed to girls' more negative expectations of sex, as well as harsher proscriptions against sex for girls than boys. However, with such widely disparate expectations of sex, how do boys and girls decide to have sex, and why do teenage girls ever have sex given their negative expectations?

Although there is much research on which demographic factors may make teens more likely to have sex, there is little on how those decisions come about. There is no research that asks why boys have sex more than girls do and why they do so earlier. Teens do not add up their demographic variables to see if they should have sex. They have sex in the context of their lives and relationships. As Brooks-Gunn and Furstenberg (1989) note "almost no information exists as to how teens initiate sexual activity."[131] From *their* perspective, how do teens decide to have sex?[132]

THE INTERACTIONAL PATHS TO SEX...

A girl's ideal love for a male peer *at adolescence* often adds a new dimension to ideal love—sex. However, this is not because the quality of a girls' ideal love has changed or become more sexual, more passionate, or more desirous, but because male peers often insist on, provoke, or encourage girls to have sex. Several working-class girls said that the pattern in their high school was that many girls often had sex in their freshmen year because older boys saw them as easy targets, taught them how to party, and convinced them to have sex. The different paths that girls and boys take to having sex are generally that girls are pressured into sex, and boys do the pressuring. Both boys and girls see this as the pattern. Fourteen-year-old Adam said, "Well, I think the boys put a lot of pressure on the girls to do it." Girls acknowledge that boys pressure girls by using love. "Boys put so much pressure on you. It's just like TV—'But I love you,' and girls just giving it up, and they shouldn't." Tiffany, beginning in the language of ideal love, said,

> It's nice to lie there in their warm, comforting arms, and if you have feel-
> ings for them it's so hard to look in their eyes and say no. I could only do
> it if I was really angry. I mean if he was forcing me I could, he'd be in for
> a fight, but if it was just like "Oh please, come on baby" no way could I
> say no.

Not all boys, especially younger boys, seem to realize that they are pressuring girls. The boys I spoke with assumed that girls, usually anonymous, generic girls—their girlfriends were the exception—wanted to have sex as much as they did. Boys told me, "Girls want to have sex, too. It's pretty much the same as boys." Or "I think they [girls] think the same thing about sex and wonder about sex and wanting to do it." However, a few middle-class boys (three) acknowledged that sex, at least at first, was not as good for girls as for boys. For example, Rick, who is fifteen and has not had sex, said, "It seems like for girls it would not be nearly as much fun, 'cause the first time is sort of nothing."

Older boys clearly do know that they are pressuring girls for sex. Anthropologist Peggy Reeve Sanday describes fraternity boys' common practice of "working a yes out." She recorded the following conversation between fraternity brothers:

> "Sometimes a woman has to resist your advances to show how sincere she
> is. And so, sometimes you've gotta help them along. You know she means
> no the first time, but the third time she could say no all night and you
> know she doesn't mean it"
> "Yeah, no always mean no at the moment, but there might be other ways
> of..."
> "Working a yes out?"
> "Yeah!"

71

"Get her out on the dance floor, give her some drinks, talk to her for a while."

"Agree to something, sign the papers…"

"And give her some more drinks!"

"Ply her with alcohol."[133]

The older boys I spoke with were not this explicit in indicating that they knew girls were sometimes reluctant. However, although both boys and girls often said that they "talked it over" with their partner before deciding to have sex, "talking it over" meant something different for boys and girls. Their descriptions of these "talks" and the tones of voices in which they spoke about them were quite different. Boys described things like middle-class fifteen-year-old, Craig did, "She was a little reluctant, but we just talked it over and decided it would be okay." Or like Scott did when I asked him, "How did you decide [to have sex]?" "It was easy after we talked it over," he replied.

Girls, however, were more reticent and much less likely to say it was easy when describing these conversations. For example, I asked the girls who had had sex the same question I asked Scott. "How did you decide to have sex?" Their answers were quite different from Scott's and most boys'. For example, Elaine, Diana, Kendra, and Jodi replied in typical ways.

It just happened really. I mean, I didn't want to 'cause I couldn't ever pic-ture myself having sex, but umm, all my friends did, and umm, so it just happened and he was my first so…I thought it was right 'cause we were going out for two years before we did.

—Elaine

How did you decided to have sex?
I don't know. We like went out for three and a half months, and that's when we did it. We just talked about it and stuff that it was gonna hurt. And it did hurt!

—Diana

How did you make that decision [to have sex]?
I don't know. Umm, it seemed kind of natural, I don't know. I just thought about it and it just kind of happened.

—Kendra

Have you had sex?
Once. [*Said in a tiny, almost inaudible voice*].
How did you decide to have sex?
Well, it just sort of happened. I don't know.

How would you decide to do it again in the future?
I don't know. It would probably just come up again.

—Jodi

Girls express their feelings of missing agency with their repeated phrase "it just happened."[134]

Cook, Boxer, and Herdt find that lesbian teens report sexual sequencing that is first heterosexual then homosexual while gay male teens report the reverse. The girls in their study also say that heterosexual sex was something that *happened to them* while it was something the gay boys sought out. The authors propose that "the greater likelihood of sexual pressure and coercion experienced by females from males predisposes girls to the heterosexual/homosexual sequence, not as a choice but as a consequence of growing up in a society where females encounter such experiences more than males."[135] I suggest that many lesbian teenagers and straight teenage girls have heterosexual sex for the same reasons—coercion.

Because the girls' answers to how they decided to have sex were often tinged with feelings of regret, shame, and hesitation, I became suspicious that many girls did not really *want* to have sex, and so I began asking boys and girls "Why do you think it is hard for some girls to say no if they really don't want to have sex?" Girls often answered this third person question in the first person or second person, moving the experience closer to themselves. Girls' answers, particularly working-class girls, reveal that their boyfriends often pressure them into sex. Notice the first and second person answers and the language of fear throughout girls' answers.

Because they'll be *scared* like, that the guy will just say forget it, and he'll just probably go off to another girl and ask them the same question. And he'll just go to a person that says yes and stay with them, and then he'll probably just do it and then leave.

—Ellen

'Cause you're afraid that they're gonna leave you.

—Amanda

'Cause they're afraid the boy won't like them anymore or something would happen, you know, he'd get mad.

—Stephanie

'Cause the boys break up with you or something like that. Or they say, "You don't love me."

—Valerie

73

Oh, it is. It is really hard [to say no]. Because some guys say "If you love me you would do it." And I mean you don't want to say no 'cause you're afraid that they're gonna break up with you if you do and you don't really want to say yes but you do anyways. I just…they do 'cause…(sigh.)

—Jodi

'Cause you don't want them to get mad at you. You don't want them to like…'Cause I did that once and he kind of got pissed 'cause he said that he'd be hurting and stuff like that. But I just didn't want to and like he wasn't…he wasn't mad at me, but he was mad at that fact that he was gonna hurt. But I know a lot of guys, like I'll be hanging out with my friends and they'll go in the other room and the guy will come out pissed off 'cause they won't.

—Danielle

[It's hard to say no] 'Cause they don't want the guy to think that she's a sissy, or she's, she's nothing, or she's not gonna be popular, or no one will think she's pretty anymore. Just for self-esteem reasons I think.

—Linda

Finally, Samantha said straightforwardly that it is hard for some girls to say no to boys "'Cause they're afraid of them."

Working-class girls openly discussed this pressure *and* the fact they often felt compelled to give in to it. A few even revealed such coercive pressure without being asked. For example, one girl told me she had sex with her boyfriend the first time when they were playing Truth or Dare with friends, and she "had to" do the dare. She was not physically forced to have sex, but goaded into it by her boyfriend (and presumably other friends who were present). The middle-class girls were more often able to say no to sex. For example, seventeen-year-old Heather told me confidently,

That decision has definitely come up in the past two relationships I've had, because those people have been a lot older and umm, especially with Joey who was the last guy I went out with, umm. He sort of forced me to make that decision really early on, we had gone out for two weeks and all of sudden he was ready to have sex and that was a natural progression for him and he assumed that I'd you know…I think that…to be in love with somebody probably comes once or twice or maybe three times in your life time and I don't believe my friends when they say they are in love with their boyfriends who they went out with for two weeks, umm, but I also don't know that you have to be *in* love with somebody, you know, to have sex with them. I think that if there's a potential for you to be in love with them and a really deep caring and definitely commitment and just feeling really comfortable with the person. Feeling like you could say anything to them, it's a pretty important prerequisite for having sex with them and I didn't feel like that with him after two weeks or after two months.

Similarly when I asked Kelly, "Why is it hard for some girls to say no to sex when they don't want to have sex?" she replied, "No problem! I mean, I really don't have any problem with that at all."

"Why do you think that others girls might?" I asked.

"I don't know, I just decided a long time ago that if this doesn't work out you know, there are a trillion other one's out there. So, I mean, I know, I know that there are,…that I will find someone someday who is perfect. And until then I don't have to deal with any of these others." Middle-class girls are better able than working-class girls to refuse sex that they do not want for several reasons. As we have seen, they remain in ideal love with their fathers longer than working-class girls do and so are less likely to feel ideal love for a male peer. This makes it easier for them to say they do not want sex. It is as if the vicarious subjectivity that they receive via their relationships with their fathers is working for them. Others also have mothers who provide them with a subjectivity that helps them to feel like they can say no to sex they do not want (but even middle-class girls rarely want to say yes). Few mothers or fathers were able to provide their daughters with desire, and no girl expressed a confident, excited wish to have sex in the ways that some boys did. Also, Heather and Kelly were not only middle-class, but they were also in their late rather than early or middle teens, and being older seems to correlate with having a greater ability to refuse sex when one does not want it.

However, middle-class girls are not immune to giving in to their boyfriends' pressure to have sex. They are more reluctant to admit doing so than working-class girls are. They tell stories of pressure to have sex that disguise the pressure and the fact they gave in to it. Kendra, an opinionated middle-class girl, who prided herself on her self-confidence and assertiveness reflected on her decision to have sex.

> How did I decide to? Umm, it just seemed kind of natural, I don't know. I mean I thought about it. It just seemed like it was right. I was fifteen…He wanted to have sex with me and I had said no, I mean I didn't feel pressure and that's not why I said I would, but looking back I think it kind of took our relationship a step further and if I hadn't I don't know what we would have done. It would have been kind of stagnated I guess.

75

"The relationship will stagnate" is another version of "He'll break up with you if you say no." It is a story that can deny that a middle-class girl is really under pressure from boys and giving in to it. Middle-class girls are more invested in this disguise than working-class girls because they know from sex education and their knowledge of feminism that being "talked into it" is not the "right" reason for having sex. Regardless of how they discuss it, both middle- and working-class girls describe a variety of ways in which they are pressured or coerced into sex by their boyfriends. Such pressure clearly does not foster sexual subjectivity.

How does this gender dynamic of boys pressuring girls for sex and girls "giving in" get set up? I suggest that much of it is a result of the differing capacities for agency and sexual subjectivity that girls and boys have constructed up until this point. Chilman suggests that there is a lack of a developmental perspective on teenage sex.[136] This is the case; the research on puberty and teen sex are two separate literatures. However, adolescents often become sexually active before they are completely "done" with puberty, and puberty is laden with meanings about sexual bodies. Puberty, as we saw, makes girls anxious about sex and their bodies and unsure of themselves and their abilities to act in the world. Puberty puts restrictions on girls' sexuality and self-confidence. Boys, on the other hand, come out of puberty feeling more grown up, more independent, and feeling generally positive about their bodies that are becoming more adult-like, and importantly, more masculine. When teens with these different capacities start dating each other, they have unequal abilities to negotiate for what they want; they have different wants; and the relationship means different things to them. Boys are more sure that they want sex, and as we have seen, they have higher expectations of sex. Girls, who are deeply invested in ideal love, are vague about when they will want sex and if they are "ready," especially since being ready rarely has anything to do with desire.

> I told him I'm not right now, that I'm not ready for it. And umm, when I'm ready I don't know if I'll still be with him, but I hope that he like understands that maybe we're not gonna have it for a while or ever.
>
> —Erin

> *How would you decide to have sex?*
> You should be ready. I just want that.
> *How would you define being ready?*
> I don't know that's hard. Umm, if this guy is like the right one and you're not gonna regret it afterwards. Be thoughtful and have a good idea.
>
> —Sondra

These feelings of unsureness make sense given girls' low expectations of sex. This psychodynamic disparity in agency and sexual subjectivity, laid upon the cultural inequalities between the genders, gives boys a greater capacity to push for what they want, and leaves girls less able to articulate what they want for themselves *and* less able to claim it forcefully (or to articulate what they don't want and forcefully refuse it). I do not suggest girls are without any agency or without any sexual subjectivity. Rather, within the interactions with her boyfriend, within the "We talked it over," a girl finds it particularly hard to hold her own against a boy's assuredness and convincing reasons. This is especially true when a girl finds herself in ideal love with this boy. It is important not to underestimate the role and power of ideal love in adolescent girls' lives. As much as sex is not about passion and lust for teen girls, it *is* about ideal love and fear of losing one's ideal love, if one refuses sex. As we have seen above, many girls make this connection, saying "He'll break up with you if you say no."

There are exceptions to this pattern. Some boys do not want to have sex (yet), and certainly did not pressure girls to. In my sample they tend to be younger, Catholic boys, or boys who wanted to be in love first (which correlates with being younger). Jim, a working-class boy, told me a story about fears of guilt and pregnancy.

> I'd just say not to have sex. Being Catholic that's basically the only opinion I hear. But...I don't know. I wouldn't really feel comfortable buying a condom anyways, and I wouldn't have sex without a condom 'cause I'd feel guilty, and I'd help out with a kid, and so I just wouldn't have sex at all.

Similarly, Brent, a middle-class boy, also was not in a hurry to have sex not because of fear or guilt but because he felt he was too young and "not ready." He was one of the only boys who used the term "ready."

> I'm definitely not ready to have sex yet...I'm not in control of my social life or academic life, and I'm not ready to start dealing with myself in that way. I'll be ready once I find somebody I love. I'm not gonna do it before that because, because my friends some of them have already done it and they feel real shitty about it if they did it with some random person just to try it or something.

Other teens in my sample also had decided to postpone sex. Some rationally thought about the decision, about their feelings, about themselves and their partners and decided not to have sex. These teens were few. (See Chapter Six.) More often the teens who decided not to have sex as teens (at least not up until the point at which I interviewed them) did so because of "morals," religion, and AIDS. For these teens the decision was usually more abstract than for those who decided to have sex, because they usually were teens who did not have "serious" girlfriends or boyfriends.

Several girls and boys also said that either because of their religion or "morals" they wanted to wait. One seventeen-year-old middle-class boy and one sixteen-year-old working-class girl who had each decided they did not want to have sex, said it was because they did not want to "get AIDS." Meghan said,

> I'm gonna wait. Like with AIDS it really scares you. I wouldn't, I would-n't do that. I'm gonna wait 'til, I don't believe in having sex before…a lot of people do it, you know what I mean…but now with everything, AIDS…

It is my impression that AIDS education has given teens who do not want to have sex, but do not want to be seen as "wimps" or "goody-goodies" an acceptable reason to decide against sex. It is more acceptable in teen culture to say one fears AIDS than to say one fears God, religion, parents, or pregnancy.

EXPERIENCES OF SEX…

As we would expect, given such different paths to sex, boys and girls have very different experiences of sex. The girls who did have sex found that it lived up to their negative expectations. They often described the experience as painful, scary, disappointing, or confusing.

> There was a couple of times that I thought I had decided and I was like "Okay, okay!" and then "No, I can't! I can't!" He was like "Okay, okay." And it was like the third time that I had said that. I'm like "Okay." I was real scared. I was afraid it would hurt. I cried and it did hurt.
>
> —Valerie

> I was fourteen. I was really nervous. I can remember shaking, and it was-n't the most intimate thing. The kid I was with was a virgin also, so we had no idea, or guidance or knowledge whatsoever about what we were doing. And we were downstairs on this couch and I was really shaking. My skirt was just pulled up and his pants down at his ankles. We just wung it. We were like "All right what the hell do we do?" It was like I can remember really brief. Not really intimate 'cause we were both scared out of our minds. I was shaking and I was just not feeling very sexual at that moment. It wasn't that great. I remember we just sat there side by

side with our hands folded afterwards. That happened so what's next? It
was mostly just silence for the rest of the night.

—Jill

Actually I was kind of happy, well, I don't know how to explain it. In a
way I felt really good because I had shared this with somebody, but it was
the most painful experience of my life.

—Tiffany

Have you had sex with him?
Yeah. He was my first, and it hurt! Very much so. We went out for like
three and a half months and that's when we did it.
How did you decide to have sex?
We just talked about it and stuff, that it was gonna hurt and stuff. 'Cause
he was like my first in almost absolutely everything. And it did hurt!

—Danielle

As Thompson notes, it is ironic that "While girls hold their lovers responsible for virtually all the emotional pain they experience in relationships, they
rarely blame them for sexual pain during first coitus. Instead they blame their
own bodies."[137] Girls' experiences were not painful and scary because of some
biological or natural necessity that first sex be bad for girls, but because girls
often have sex when they do not physically or emotionally desire it, when
they have little experiential knowledge about what sex will be like, how they
will feel and how their bodies will feel. Girls' later and less frequent masturbation than boys contributes to their lack of subjective sexual body knowledge. Women who masturbate have better sex with their partners.[138] Finally,
many girls move from kissing to intercourse in an extremely short period of
time. Petting or "all the stuff that comes before" is often not a significant part
of girls' sexual experiences. Jill said she was a tomboy and thought kissing was
"gross" when she thirteen, but she had sex when she fourteen. This leaves little time to learn about sexual pleasure. As Erin told me,

> I think it's basically that guys think that…like that sex, is like the way to
> get…is like what you should do, you should have sex even if you haven't
> done everything else, even if you're not like totally comfortable, I think
> that they think that it's just like something they have to do. And you
> know, girls just like want to take their time and take it slowly and go for
> everything, like that leads up to sex and things like that.

Tolman finds that two thirds of her sample of thirty girls said that they
"experienced sexual desire."[139] However, Tolman did not interview boys, and

79

it is unclear if the extent of these girls' desires would be equal to that of boys similarly sampled. Would what "counts" as desire be more narrowly defined if researchers listened to boys as well? Also, we must distinguish between sexual desire and sexual pleasure. Although teen girls may desire, few find sexual pleasure. Thompson found that only one fourth of her sample of 400 girls were "pleasure narrators." "The pleasure narrators describe taking sexual initiative; satisfying their own sexual curiosity; instigating petting and coital relations"[140] Lesbian teens were more likely to be pleasure narrators (when discussing sex with girls) than heterosexual teens were in her sample. However, even they are rare as most lesbians do not come out until their late teens or early twenties.[141]

I did not find as many pleasure narrators as Thompson did, perhaps because my sample of girls was not as broad. Kristen who had waited a "long time" (until she was sixteen) before having sex said that she was "just a bundle of joy" afterward because she was "so excited to call [her best friend] and just so psyched." A few girls, especially those who were older and middle-class, said that sex was "better" or a "little better" after the first few times. Fullilove et al. also find that sex gets better for girls as they get older. The authors found that among poor black women, age was related to having more power in sexual communication, in being clear about what one wants, and in getting it.[142] In my study, Jill an eighteen-year-old working-class girl, described her current sex life as pleasurable, although her sex at ages fourteen and fifteen was not. However, she focused her discussion on the relationship rather than on desire or physical pleasure.

> It's gotten a lot better! It's good. Ummm, I don't really know how to say this. Sex is like a bonus, you know. It's another way of bringing us closer, but it's not in any way the center point or the main point of the relationship. We just consider it something extra special in the relationship.

Cherri, a middle-class nineteen-year-old, now had orgasms (she was one of only three girls who said she did), and she too attributed it to the fact of "love." Cherri said, "As soon as I began to relax and trust, it happened. We have a really open communication kind of relationship, and that makes all the difference. We're really close." Finally, Audrey, a middle-class sixteen-year-old, said that she was more physical than her boyfriend.

> I had a serious boyfriend. We went out for like four months. He was sweet and funny, and he thought I was pretty. But, I couldn't get him to talk to me. He was very quiet and closed off. He was also very clingy emotionally. It was sort of the opposite of the usual stereotype. He was more emotionally dependent and I was more physical.

What do you mean you were more physical?
I wanted to be touching and doing physical stuff more than he did and I
wanted to go further sometimes.

Even these girls did not wholeheartedly embrace sexual experience and
expressed a lot of ambivalence. For example, Audrey used an interesting strategy to resist having sex with her boyfriend. She decided that she and her
boyfriend were going to have sex, and so wanting to be "responsible" she went
to the doctor to get birth control pills. However, somewhere between starting
the pills and sleeping with her boyfriend, she "cheated" on him. Cheating here
means that she went out with another boy and kissed (and maybe petted), not
that she had sex with him. Audrey then thought that since she had "cheated"
on her boyfriend she must not be "ready" to have sex yet, and so decided not
to. Kristen admitted to using the same strategy at one time as well. While
strategies like "cheating" allow girls to assert control over their sexuality in an
exciting way, they also express the ambivalence teenage girls, even girls who
have "decided" to have sex, feel about sex.

Boys did not rave about their actual experiences of sex, but gave mild
answers that claimed it was as they expected. They were much less negative
and less ambivalent about their experiences than girls were, and they seemed
less self-reflective. Scott said, "It was good. I was psyched to have done it."
Craig only said, "I couldn't believe I saw a completely naked female body."
Michael said with less confidence, "I felt okay. I kind of hoped I did okay. I
didn't really know, you know, if she thought it was *[okay]*." These answers were
typical of boys in general and boys of their class. Middle-class boys descriptions were slightly less confident and less positive.

Moffatt found in his research on sex among undergraduates that college
men discussed sexual pleasure very little in their narrative descriptions of sex
because "The male subtext on sexual pleasure was, in all probability, 'Of *course*,
I enjoy sex. I'm a normal guy. It goes without saying!'"[143] This, I suspect, is
why boys in my sample said little about pleasure specifically, but also did not
tell stories of pain or disappointment as girls did. Discussion of boys' pleasure
from sex arose only in the context of discussions about condoms. Both boys
and girls claimed that often boys did not want to use condoms because as one
middle-class boy claimed, "You can't feel anything." In discussing with Amy
whether students would use condoms if they were made available in school,
she said sympathizing with the boys, "I don't know if they would [use con-
doms]. 'Cause a lot of guys, I know don't like them. 'Cause they don't get
enough satisfaction off them." While boys and some girls expressed concern
about boys' lack of or lessened pleasure, there was little concern about girls'
lack of pleasure. It was expected that girls would not like sex as much as boys,
especially first sex.

SEX AND SEXUAL SUBJECTIVITY...

What are the effects of first and early sexuality on teenage girls' and boys' selves? The sexual experiences that most boys have cause them to feel more subjective, agentic, and more like sexual subjects. The experience of girls "giving in" to boys solidifies boys' feelings of agency and sexual subjectivity. A boy now feels like he can will things and make them happen. He can do, and do sexually.

Boys feel grown up and more masculine as a result of having sex. Sex has often been seen as the test of masculinity for men, as a "mainstay of identity."[144] Heterosexual sex also facilitates bonds between men. Teenage boys know that having sex makes them more masculine. In April of 1993 the media focused attention on a group of boys in suburban southern California who called themselves the "Spur Posse." (They were fans of the San Antonio Spurs.) These boys were in competition with each other to see who could have sex with the most girls. Each time they achieved orgasm with a different girl was a "point." These boys went on several television talk shows defending their competition and bragging about how many points they had. A nineteen-year-old was the highest scorer, with sixty-six points. Eight of these boys were arrested on various felony rape and sexual assault charges, but all were released except one boy who had allegedly had sex with a ten-year-old girl. Parents (especially fathers) met these stories with a "boys will be boys attitude." One father said, "Nothing my boy did was anything any red-blooded American boy wouldn't do at his age." One son said, "My dad used to brag to his friends. All the dads did. When we brought home girls they liked, they'd say cool, and tell their buddies...It's all the moms that are freaking out about this stuff. But that's probably that Freudian thing. You know, penis envy." However, one boy's mother said, "What can you do? It's a testosterone thing."[145] I use this extreme example to suggest that for teenage boys having sex brings status, and, in particular, masculine status, even in this distorted form.

The boys I interviewed did not describe anything like "The Spur Posse," perhaps because this story is extreme, or perhaps because boys tell different stories about sex to each other, to men, than they do to women. However, their discussions, especially working-class boys', did indicate that sex made them feel grown-up, masculine, and bonded with other men, and they did indicate that bragging and boasting about sex was part of teenage boy culture.

Many boys described what happens after sex to be talking about it or in some way conveying it to other boys. When I asked Scott if he told anyone after he had sex he said, "You don't really have to come out and tell your friends, they just sort of know. You kinda just give the impression." Similarly, Jack and Alex said, after sex boys tell others they "did it," and Jack, in particular, says boys in fact "do it" to gain status from their friends.

> Boys do it so they can go tell their friends, "Yeah, Yeah!" You know.
> Although if it's your girlfriend you don't go tell your friends about it, but
> if it's like Sally off the Street then, yeah, you do.
>
> —Jack

> 'Cause there are two things that guys talk about when they get together.
> Girls, sex, and sports. Those are the only things they have in common.
> Girls and sex are one.
>
> —Alex

Some boys even "discussed" it with their fathers, thus making them truly feel
grown up. Their fathers confirm the importance of sex and women to masculinity.

> Everybody talks about it. It's like…"Yeah, I did her, I did this!" Or let's
> see "I screwed her." We generally do talk about it a lot. It's our nature. My
> father says when you stop looking [at women] then it's time for the grave.
>
> —Paul

Researchers have examined how parental attitudes and parent-child interactions affects teenagers' likelihood of having sex,[146] and interesting here is the
finding that mothers' discussions of sex with sons and daughters lead to later
intercourse but fathers' discussions with sons lead to earlier intercourse.[147]

For many boys, having sex may also relieve fears that they are not masculine enough, that they are a "faggot," a "wimp," a "sissy," a "baby," a "girl." No
boy said this to me explicitly about himself, but many said sex was important
for the masculinity of other boys. For example, Dennis, a middle-class fifteen-
year-old, said, "I think for a lot of guys it looks macho and stuff to have, to be
having sex." And, recall Jack's comment which he made with swinging fists,
that boys do it so they can tell their friends "Yeah! Yeah!" Having sex may be
proof to oneself and others of masculinity. It is an accomplishment. Girls, like
Jill, also described sex as an accomplishment for boys.

> If you're sitting around a table with guys, which happens, they're waiting
> around for some guy and he's late and his excuse is that he was getting
> "laid" or having sex, or whatever, it's okay. You know. If you're scoring
> with a girl or however, they want to term it, they just look at it as an
> achievement or an accomplishment. That's not all of them, but you know,
> that's part of it. But for girls, most of us are "Oh, I'm in love, and stuff like
> that." Love and commitment are important for girls and for boys they
> look at it as an accomplishment.

Similarly, Jack told me that if he were to talk to his younger brother about sex he would tell him to use condoms and that the girl would "never stop calling him," but he would also "cheer him on a little." Thus, first and early experiences of sex lead boys to develop bonds with other men, masculinity, more agency and sexual subjectivity, and recognition for all these things from others.

By contrast, first and early experiences of sex generally lessen girls' feelings of subjectivity, agency, and sexual subjectivity. To restate—girls' first experiences of sex are usually negative. They say things like, "It was the most painful experience of my life." After sex girls often feel confused and unsure of themselves, their "decisions," their bodies, and sex. Many girls describe this confusion which may take several forms from fear of pregnancy, betrayal of friends and family, uncertainty about one's body. Kendra felt badly about herself for not having used contraception, and she was afraid she might be pregnant.

> *Did you use contraception the first time?*
> (Breathes in deeply.) No. Which is really bad, and I knew it, and I was just like praying 'cause I, I mean I had sex ed. since I was in like third grade, and I knew that…it's not like I thought "Oh, your first time you can't get pregnant." But I was just like…and I thought I was pregnant, but then I got my period, but that was very stressful. I was like ready to go buy one of those pregnancy tests. Or I was like, Sherri, one of my good friends, she was like, "Okay, we're going to the pharmacy," and I was like "No, I don't want to go." But I wasn't [pregnant].[148]

84

Tiffany was in the midst of her confusion about sex when we talked. She felt betrayed by her body, her family, and her friends. Her tone as she talked at length about her experience of sex moved between solemn and frustrated.

> We'd been going out a long time. And, we just felt that it was the right thing to do. We were gonna be responsible, definitely. And it was really a hard decision to make, because his parents are really Catholic, but they're not really much as Catholics—but like his mother, any girl that has a boyfriend, and she sleeps with him in her mind is a slut. And that's the way he's been brought up. He doesn't really agree with it. That made it really hard 'cause she was calling me a slut because I used a tampon. She found it in the garbage can and that made me so mad. I couldn't believe it. And that's so untrue and I don't know where she got that because you can still be a virgin and be using a tampon, and at that time I was. If she ever found out [that we were having sex now], I don't know what would really happen. We just made a decision because we felt that we love each other…I know I made the right decision. [But] it's really a hard test when

you've got people saying well did you? Especially my mother, she goes and takes me to Planned Parenthood and then she says "I feel like shit for taking you there." She can't deal with the fact that I'm on the pill. I mean she knows this guy and she thinks he's really nice and all, and it's just that she can't cope with it. It's not the way she was brought up. I can understand that, but it's also hard when you've got his side of the family and getting that view. I think the worst part was when I didn't get my period on time, that was a major scare for me. That really hurt. [Unlike many girls this girl used foam and condoms when she first had sex]. I don't know what's worse, knowing that you could be pregnant or knowing that you could have an infection. Because it makes you think, did I make the right decision having sex? There are so many problems that come with it. You know my parents didn't know when I first started having sex and then they found out and at first they were really nice about it because we all thought that I was pregnant at that time, and they were like "No one should have to go through this." And after that it was just like, it was weird, it was kind of like this permission, and everything makes you second guess yourself. And now, I just had a period, a really long, horrible period, now I've got this other one that's just not going away, and now I think I've got some type of infection. Nobody knows, except a couple friends, and my parents don't know and it kind of makes everything so much more complicated. I wake up tired. It makes me feel in a way like a slut. I know that I shared something with somebody that I loved, but now, I feel so disgusting. I think that's what kids need to be told—it's not just STD's and everything, but all these things that go along with it, the mental stress, my mom told me, and I didn't really believe her. I wouldn't not do it again. I would do it again. I don't feel bad about that, but I never knew. It just makes it so horrible, it takes away from the actual act of sex. I don't think it's sex that's so bad, it's everything else that's horrible. If anything that would stop me from doing it again because the mental worry is so hard and you know, before I had sex I was thinking this is the last time this person is gonna see me as a virgin. I was like, what I was doing in my mind was horrible. It was hard 'cause my parents aren't liberal people, and I wish that most kids wouldn't have to go through that, and we wouldn't have to go sneaking around to some motel, we wouldn't have to lie about what you did that day. You wouldn't have to feel bad. All I want is for them to respect me. If I'm gonna feel good about myself I can't do it all on my own, and that's what I'm having trouble with right now.

Much of Tiffany's story reveals another longstanding complexity of sex for girls. If one has sex, does she become a "slut" or a "'ho'"? The double standard in sex is still firmly rooted in teenage culture. In fact, Ward and Taylor write of their research,

> Across six ethnic groups one observation was strikingly similar; all respondents introduced the universal theme of a double standard toward sexual behavior that is limiting and oppressive to females. In all groups, boys were generally allowed more freedom and were assumed to be more sexually active than girls.[149]

Girls, as well as boys in my sample, subscribe to this double standard, although many middle-class girls did note that it exists and is unfair. Erin critically told me,

> It's very different for boys, it's like "a good job" if they have sex with somebody and then they're rewarded and stuff and all the guys are just like "That's great!" You have sex, and you're a girl and it's like "Slut!" That's how it is and you know guys can like sleep around and stuff, even if it's dangerous, but girls—you do that and it's just like, it's not accepted. I think that's really warped since it take two people to have sex. It's very different.

In general, however, girls and boys distinguish between "Sally off the Street" and a "girlfriend" or between "the real cross-your-legs type girls and your so-called sluts," and there are no such distinctions made for boys. Although some girls are trying to create one by now referring to boys who treat girls badly and are only out for sex as "himbos," an alternative to bimbos. Many girls, like Tiffany, take the distinction of slut to heart and fear it. This is why ideal love is so important. If one has sex for love, she is not a slut, at least among these girls.

The meaning of slut, however, is highly variable and has changed somewhat in recent decades. Among the girls in my sample, simply having premarital sex was not enough to get labeled a slut, unless one was "too young" even in the eyes of peers to be having sex (consensus seemed to be that twelve or thirteen, pre-high school, was too young). Having multiple partners more often constitutes what one girl called "slut behavior." Similarly, Fullilove et al. (1990) in focus group discussions about sexuality with poor black women and teenage girls found that the definition of a "bad girl" was based on "sexual aggression; 'looseness,' that is giving sex in a casual manner without regard for who the partner was or requiring anything of the relationship; and 'tossing,' that is, giving sex in exchange for money or drugs."[150] Similarly, the girls whom I interviewed made distinctions between "regular" or "normal" girls and "girls who want it all the time," girls who "have it [sex] just to have it," and girls who "just do it to get in with the crowd, to be popular." Sociologist Ruth Horowitz in her study of urban Chicano youth found that girls who had sex before marriage were seen as "loose women," if they could not regain esteem by establishing themselves as mothers.[151] Regardless of its particular contextual meaning, the word slut holds a lot of power. Being called a slut or a ho—or feeling like one—is to feel degraded and dirty. Thus, this double standard adds to feelings of confusion after sex.

The feelings of confusion and uncertainty about sex span a wide range of time. Kendra and Tiffany describe these feelings in the weeks following sex. Elaine, on the other hand, felt confused and scared *immediately* after sex. I wondered if she had been more coerced than other girls or simply more willing to describe her feelings immediately following sex.

> I was kind of just like confused. I didn't know what to do. You know, I'd never had had it so, I just, I was…I went to the bathroom. I didn't know what to do, I didn't know, you know, I was really scared. I didn't know what, I didn't know what was supposed to happen or anything like that so…Now that he left I wish that we never did.

Later when I asked Elaine what advice she would give to a younger girl who was trying to decide whether or not to have sex she replied adamantly, "Don't have it! I'd just tell them to wait until they're ready, you know. Don't rush into anything 'cause once you do, it's like, it's gone, you don't have anything." This feeling that one has nothing left after sex, is one that several girls expressed. They seemed to have felt they had lost some part of their selves. This expression also suggests how much girls see sex as boys taking something from them and not as a give-and-take or a two way interaction that should be enjoyable for both people.

Thus, as Kendra's, Tiffany's and Elanie's stories demonstrate, after sex, a girl often does not know if sex is something she willed and made happen, if it was something she wanted or not. She feels unsure about her role in its occurrence. Gavey finds that some adult women have sex under similar conditions because it is easier than continuing to say no or because they sometimes fear being raped.[152] Teen girls certainly do not call what happened to them rape. In fact they often have a hard time defining the pressure they felt. As seen above, they were more willing to talk about it in the third person than in the first person. For a girl, acknowledging the coercive context in which she had sex admits to her lack of agency and makes her feel bad, whereas claiming to have wanted sex denies her actual experience of coming to have sex and of the sex itself. On the other hand, saying she wanted to have sex might leave her labeled a slut. Thus, girls often reduced the story to "It just happened."

87

NARRATIVE WORK...

In order to manage such bad and conflicting feelings, girls tell stories, or do what I came to call narrative work, in order to try to make sense of their experiences of sex. Teenage girls use narrative work as a strategy for feeling better about confusing and disappointing sexual experiences. Part of what makes first sexual experiences so difficult is that girls must negotiate between several levels of scripts. Narrative work is shaped by cultural scripts or scenarios, interpersonal scripts, and intrapsychic scripts.[153] These scripts provide girls with stories of what sex is supposed to be like. On one hand, most cultural scripts claim that sex is good, magical, romantic. On the other hand, interpersonally, and collectively, teenage girls construct a multitude of scripts for first sex. These scripts claim that first sex hurts, that one should have sex if she is in love and should not if she is not, that sex is a way to keep a boyfriend. Narrative work also takes into account the teenage girls' own wishes and fantasies about sex. Finally, when in engaging in narrative work a teenage girl tells a story about what happened that takes into account all of these scripts *and* the experience of the event—sex. Because these scripts and the experience are so often in conflict with each other, it is a difficult task to negotiate between these. Narrative work is an attempt to reconcile these contradictory feelings and scripts about "deciding" to have sex. It is a method of balancing what happened, how things are "supposed" to happen (according to cultural and interpersonal scripts), and how one wants them to be. Narrative work also manages experience as well as emotion.[154]

The finding that teen girls do narrative work is significant in light of recent theorizing and research by Brown and Gilligan.[155] Brown and Gilligan argue that at adolescence girls' "real" or "authentic" knowledge about the world and about gender inequalities goes "underground." They claim that girls silence the truth of their experiences and forget what they know, in favor of a normative discourse. Girls are subjected to a "tyranny of nice and kind," according to Brown and Gilligan. This means that they tell positive, unconflictual stories about their experiences, painting themselves and others as "nice and kind."

My data suggests, instead, that while girls sometimes cast positive light on a bad experience, they generally have little problem recalling the negative "truth" of the experience. They are not silenced. They are able to hold in tension both the negative "truth" of the experience and a more positive version of the experience that allows them some agency and to tell a less conflict-ridden story. Brown and Gilligan also hear these conflicted stories,[156] but they see girls as always losing the battle for authenticity. This is because Brown and Gilligan are themselves deciding which narrative, of the many the girls are telling, is true. They do not tell the reader how they make these decisions, but they seem to think they know what the "real" feelings and "real" selves and "real" experiences of these girls are. I do not think we can make such distinctions.

In general, girls have to do much narrative work in order to feel okay about their sexual experiences. Working-class girls' experiences elicit more narrative work than middle-class girls'. Because middle-class girls have more subjective knowledge, more information about sex, and because they tend to be slightly older when they first have sex, their experiences of sex are not as negative as working-class girls' are and thus do not elicit narrative work as frequently.

In general, I suspect that audiences for these managed stories about sex were girls' friends as well as themselves. As Thompson writes,

> Most teenage girls value friends a great deal. They are the essential audience for the talk about family, sex, and romance—the "you" in girls' most frequent phrase "you know," and the only therapists or counselors most girls have, their main line to comfort, advice, encouragement, and relief.[157]

Girls also used narrative work to convince themselves and me in the course of our interviews that they had not been coerced into sex, as this girl did.[158]

> We were going out for a while, and we just, we were downstairs, and I don't know…It's kinda like, he's kinda like, not a sexual person, but you know…all guys how they are. We just…I wasn't forced into it or anything. I wanted to, it was just I was worried…I don't mind. But like my mother was upstairs, and I was like "no, not here! My mother'll come down." You know, so it was kinda planned, not really but it was…It wasn't really what I expected, but it wasn't bad. It was like "that's what I've waited for?"

"I was worried," and "I don't mind," instead of "I wanted to," reveal that this girl was unsure about having sex. "All guys you know how they are," and "I was like 'No, not here!…'" suggest that she was pressured to have sex by her boyfriend. She also felt unsure about her experience—"It wasn't really what I expected"—and disappointed—"That's what I've waited for?" Yet not wanting to feel completely without agency or sexual subjectivity, she cannot bring herself to say outright that she was unsure and pressured to have sex. Instead she says, wanting me to understand, "You know, so it was kinda planned, not really but it was…"

Danielle struggled with similar confusing sexual experiences, and tells a similar contradictory story.

89

> I regretted it kind of, kind of. We tried like five times and we couldn't
> 'cause it killed so bad. It was like Aaahhh! I love him, I'm glad I did it,
> but...No. I felt bad because I felt like I was a slut for some reason. I just
> felt real bad about it. But, well, it changed our relationship. It kind of
> broke the ice, but we had kind of already broke through it, you know. It
> just made us a lot closer. I don't know. I could tell it was different the day
> after, when we were together and stuff.

She vacillates between regret and gladness about having sex, between feeling like a slut and feeling like sex made them closer. The one thing she is clear
about is that sex hurt. She weaves these feelings into a narrative that helps her
to maintain some feelings of agency and sexual subjectivity. This narrative
claims her experience of regret and pain, but also claims that she affected
change by having sex (she made her relationship "closer") and that she made
the right sexual decision (she was glad to have had sex because she loved him).
These last two claims concur with both cultural and interpersonal scenarios.

Other girls, like Jodi and Valerie, managed their feelings the same way as the
girl above vacillating between describing the negative and digging up something positive about their sexual experiences.

> I was sore...I felt different. I can't explain the feeling, but I sort of felt dif-
> ferent inside, you know...Like, I didn't know if I wanted to go out with
> him anymore...I just felt weird.
> *Do you think that it changed anything in your relationship?*
> I think it brought us closer together.
>
> —Jodi

> It wasn't as bad as I thought it would be. I didn't really feel comfortable
> with it, but then, I got to feel a little better about it. It made us closer.
>
> —Ellen

Finally, here is Kristen's story who said earlier in the interview that she
would only have sex if she was "ready," "totally, totally, totally in love," and sixteen years old. Her sister had told her if she adhered to these "morals" then
she would have a good first sexual experience, and she would not get used.
Here is what she said about first intercourse.

> We started dating since I was in fifth grade, and we dated every single year
> and, umm, he always said "We're gonna have sex our freshmen year," but
> I didn't. This year when we started going out, we just...we've always had
> something going and umm, I like, if I was going out with someone else
> I'd always cheat on him with Jim (laughs). This year when we started

90

going out, we went out for a while, and we like totally, totally, totally, we were like, we were in love, and we loved each other. And it was, like, I mean, I've gone out with so many guys, but like, you know, you just know. And umm, we went to a hotel room, and he asked me real sweetly [she says in a sweet voice and makes eyes] and you know then we had sex and it was awesome, like you just have to be totally ready. Like my friends said, "It's horrible, you're gonna cry, it's gonna kill you, you're not gonna enjoy yourself." I think it's just 'cause I waited so long and I was so ready, because it didn't hurt, well yeah, it did, but umm, it hurt but it wasn't horrible, I didn't cry. It was awesome.

"We went to a hotel room and he asked me real sweetly" provides evidence that she is having great sex because, as she said earlier in the interview, she and her peers believed that "you shouldn't go out with guys that don't treat you right." Then she shows that she was right to follow her "morals" adding, "You know, then, we had sex and it was awesome, like you just have to be totally ready." However, she describes the physical experience, "because it didn't hurt, well yeah, it did…" "It hurt, but it wasn't horrible, I didn't cry," holds together the whole story. It hurt but she did not cry like her friends did, therefore her experience was different from the experiences of her friends who did not wait and who had bad experiences. Her experience "was awesome." Kristen's definition of "awesome" sex is sex that does not hurt enough to make you cry. This story manages her many feelings and lets her balance the pain of sex, peer discourses, and the conviction that she had made the right decision by having sex when she was "ready," "in love" and sixteen years old. It helps her to build many ambivalent feelings into a story that claims she has some sexual subjectivity, when she was not feeling entirely sexually subjective. Thus, narrative work is a strategy girls use to help maintain some sense of sexual subjectivity and agency in themselves after sex has left them feeling unsure of their ability to act with respect to their bodily, sexual selves.

In sum, first and early experiences of sex have different psychological outcomes (as well as material outcomes) for teenage boys and girls. Sexual experience for boys often results in them feeling grown up, masculine, bonded with other men, agentic, and sexually subjective. It is much more difficult for teenage girls to achieve such a positive outcome. Their first and early experiences of sex usually result in feeling confused, unsure of themselves and their bodies, and unclear about whether or not they did or can act agentically. Early experiences of sex, like puberty, make girls feel less sexually subjective and boys more.

"YOU COULD JUST TAKE ME AND FLIP IT OVER"

Parents and Adolescent Selves

HOW DO patterns of parental identification facilitate or hinder the development of agency and sexual subjectivity at adolescence? Psychoanalytic theory[159] suggests that identifications with parents strongly affect the self, agency, and sexual subjectivity of children. In particular, Benjamin suggests that in early childhood identification with the father allows sexual subjectivity, but only for boys, for fathers do not recognize girls.[160] She also suggests that the lack of a subjective mother makes it doubly difficult for girls to achieve subjectivity and desire. I propose that although early childhood is an important stage, development does not end there.[161] In particular, adolescence is a key moment for the establishment of agency and sexual subjectivity.

Generally the patterns of parental identification that feminist psychoanalytic theory proposes for early childhood hold in adolescence. However, these patterns are complicated by class. In particular, middle-class girls are able to identify partially with both father and mother, and they receive some recognition from both parents for some of their accomplishments. Thus, middle-class girls achieve more agency than working-class girls, although less than boys. Working-class girls are least able to derive agency and sexual subjectivity from parents because parents (and others) often do not recognize their accomplishments in realms other than beauty and femininity. Boys, both working-class and middle-class, are best able to construct agency and sexual subjectivity as they go through adolescence because of their strong identifications with their fathers. However, I also examine boys' relations with their mothers (a theme that Benjamin does not address, but that Chodorow does, although not at adolescence).[162] I describe how these relationships often feel like a hindrance to agency and masculinity for adolescent boys.

BOYS...

Boys identify with their fathers, especially the further they get into their teens. Through this identification boys come to feel like subjects who can do and act. Boys generally prefer their fathers to their mothers. Many simply said they liked their fathers more. Many boys claimed that they and their fathers were alike, that they agreed with each other on values or political issues or who was going to win the Super Bowl, and that they liked each other. Also, boys connect a sense of agency to fathers but not to mothers. Boys said their fathers gave them both more freedom and less freedom than their mothers did. In either case, they saw their fathers as more active than their mothers and often liked and respected them for it. Jim, a working-class fourteen-year-old, thinks his father gives him more independence than his mother does. He also "agrees" or identifies with his father.

> My father is, he doesn't get as mad at some things [as my mother], but when he does get mad, he gets mad. He's not violent or anything, but he's able to control it and stuff. He coaches my brother's team and he did when I was in Little League. I don't blame him he doesn't want to coach Pony League or anything. I think Little League would be fine. But, he has a lot of opinions, usually I agree with him, and he lets me do a lot more than I think my mother does.

Similarly, Doug, a middle-class seventeen-year-old, "likes" his father more.

> Umm, he's ah, I like him a lot. He's very, he's very umm, ah, as a person he's I guess pretty warm. I think that some of his faults are that he's sort of like a know it all. Umm, no matter what, he's an expert on the topic. I like him a lot better than I do my mother. I have a much better rela-

tionship with him I think. So I think he's a much better person to be around.

Thus, boys say that their fathers "let them do more" or that they "get more done" because their fathers (unlike their mothers) keep them on the straight and narrow. Brent, a middle-class fifteen-year-old, told me the entire story of his father's life in animated detail. Here is an abbreviated version of it.[163]

> *Tell me about your father.*
> Oh my God, my dad is sort of a character. Well his dad was an asshole and beat him when he was a kid. He was some ironworker racist guy, steel-worker whatever. So my dad has a real problem with authority. Oh God, he's changed over the years so I'll go through it. He ah, well he was sort of a hippie when hippie times came around. He was attractive so he had a good time with girls. He went to Vietnam basic training and then ran away when it was time for Vietnam. I don't know, something happened and he couldn't be a conscientious objector so he just left and hid out in the hills and became a hippie and grew pot and stayed with his brother and all that, and then he met my mom...And they got married. And had me and my dad worked and my mom just raised me. She married when she was eighteen or nineteen and had me when she was twenty. They realized they were pretty different and had a real hard time splitting up 'cause my dad just loves me like crazy, and didn't want to go away from us, didn't want to leave us, and so it was a long divorce...Anyway now, he's in real estate, and he's real funny. He has the same sense of humor that me and my brother do. He's sort of a kid that never grew up...We're just a lot alike!
> *Do you get along with him?*
> I get along with him really well. I don't have enough time to even miss him during the week which is sort of sad, but I know he misses me a lot. It's also sort of sad 'cause I've always seen him as perfect, perfectly fun and nice...And I forget the question.

Brent's detailed history of his father's life and their relationship was filled with emotion and a sense that he really knew his father. It provides a strong depiction of identification. In particular, the excitement that he expresses over the fact that he and his father are "a lot alike," that his father is "a kid that never grew up," and that he, his brother, and father have "the same sense of humor" echoes the excitement that Benjamin finds in the two-year-old whose mother told him "'You and Daddy are as alike as two peas in a pod,' to which the boy fervently replied, 'Say it again, Mommy!'"[164] Thus, fathers are able to rec-

95

ognize boys' agency and subjectivity. This includes their sexual subjectivity, as we will see in the following chapters.

Mothers play a different role than fathers in boys' self-development. In general, boys are less able than girls to see their mothers as people rather than as mothers. Boys tended not to identify with their mothers, and only one pointed out the similarities between himself and his mother. Depending on their ages, most described their mothers either as their caretaker or as someone with whom to disidentify.

Younger boys are still attached to their mothers as "mom," as a caretaker who fulfills their needs. They are also not separated from their mothers psychologically. These younger boys talked about how their mothers affected them and how they affected their mothers. In particular, they talked about the routines of daily life and how their mothers cared for them or failed in caring for them. Young boys often described the mundane details of their daily life with their mother and her caretaking. Here Jim, who was working-class and fourteen years old, clearly echoes Benjamin's descriptions of mothers as holding and fathers as outside and exciting.

> Well, my mother's like, well, it's kind of typical, you wait for your father to come home, so you kind of enjoy him more 'cause you don't see him as much and your mother is the one who has to yell at you the most 'cause she is around you the most…She drives everybody all over the place and sometimes the pressure gets to her 'cause with three kids in the family. Everyday I have practice, my brother probably has a game, my sister has Brownies, and she just has to drive all over the place and I wish she didn't 'cause then I could get home a lot earlier…I don't mind doing it occasionally, but I haven't been able to keep up with my homework as much because I'm just exhausted by the end of the day. Sometimes I just don't like what my mother gives me to eat so I just like have, like crackers or whatever, and then I'm starved. The sandwiches that she gives me, they just kind of like, they're awful by the time it gets to lunch, then by the end of the day I'm starved.

Sometimes younger boys described what Chodorow and Contratto call the fantasy of the perfect mother, like Ted, a middle-class fifteen-year-old, did.[165]

> My mom is, well talent-wise she's pretty similar to me. She's verbal and she's intuitive, and she's totally devoted to me and my brother and sister, and umm, she doesn't spoil us with like stuff, but she spoils us with concern because she's always worrying about what we're doing…like when

I was thinking about school decisions, I get so worried she wouldn't sleep at all, all night, and I slept like a baby. And so that's the way she is…

Older boys, however, disidentify with their mothers. They expressed more dislike for and hostility toward their mothers. Chodorow suggests that in early childhood a boy must renounce his mother (and her femininity) in order to establish masculinity.[166] While Chodorow considers the period of adolescence for girls, her model does not examine adolescence for boys. Adolescence is a time when gender norms become highly salient both internally for the self as its body changes and socially, as peer groups and adults demand even more rigid gender behavior. My research suggests that repudiation of the mother and femininity is very strong at adolescence. As teenage boys get older, there is more and more pressure to be masculine. One's attachment to his mother psychologically[167] and practically gets in the way of masculinity. Attachment to one's mother makes a boy a "mama's boy."[168] As one working-class nineteen-year-old boy told me, "When you're a teenage boy, you don't even want to have a mother." No other boy expressed this quite so overtly, but older boys' descriptions of their mothers expressed much irritation and dislike. For example,

> *Tell me about your mother.*
> Umm, she's not too strict, and she's really not enforcing. I can get away with a lot. I can use that to my advantage a lot. She won't enforce rules or anything. She seems kind of naive to me, to some of the things I do with friends and that kind of thing. My father's more the enforcer. With him around I can get things done.
> —Craig, middle-class sixteen-year-old.

97

Brad, a middle-class seventeen-year-old boy, who was calm and thoughtful most of the interview became more lively and aggressive when I asked him to tell me about his mother.

> Umm, well I think she's pretty manipulative. She's umm, I mean she's very, like what she believes and things she'll want to hold on to what she believes in even if it doesn't make any rational sense or anything. My mother is from Greece. Like a lot of times we're talking about things that even if the Greek way is not that great she'll stick to that way 'cause she just wants to defend it. We just don't get along. We fight about everything. I don't know. I guess what frustrates me about her is that like there's no logical way to make her understand something. Like having a conversation with her sometimes you'll say, "You just contradicted yourself" and

she'll say like, "No I didn't," and just avoid it or something. It's very annoying.

Brad's tone was filled with disdain. His disdain is anchored in his mother's irrationality and seeming lack of logical thinking. Rationality and logic are two highly prized traits of masculinity, especially for middle-class boys, and especially for Brad, who spent much of the interview discussing the computer war games he played and his prowess in science. In adolescence, as masculinity becomes ever more important to the self and the peer group, renouncing mother and her feminine qualities of irrationality and illogic feels necessary for boys.

GIRLS...

Middle-class girls try to and are partially able to identify with their fathers through ideal love. Ideal love, like the identificatory love that boys express for their fathers, is the result of the same process of attempting to identify with the father. Although an alienated form of identification and recognition, it affords middle-class adolescent girls some agency. Contratto finds a similar phenomenon in adult women who have fast-track careers (although difficult heterosexual love relationships) who idealized their fathers as children.[169] Much of middle-class teenage girls' discussions of their fathers reflects this ideal love and their attempt or wish to be like their fathers. They also express that their fathers encourage them to accomplish things, to be agentic, particularly in academics. Kendra, a middle-class sixteen-year-old, described her father this way.

> He's really funny. He's really smart. He loves his work. It's like the greatest thing. He's really smart, he's...I don't know, like a really good guy. He's really fair and he's pretty moral like. Yeah. I've always been kind of like his little girl and in the sense that he's told me since I was like, well as young as I can remember that I was going to do great things, and that I'm talented you know, from here to Nevada and all this stuff. I think that because he is so proud of me that sometimes I feel a lot of pressure from him. Like my term paper, I got an A and I was all excited like, and he was like "Oh, can I read it?" and I gave it to him to read and he took out a red pen and he corrected things and he said, "If you had done this like two weeks before, you could have polished it and gotten an A+," so stuff like that.

Similarly, Heather, a middle-class seventeen-year-old, says her father wants her to excel, and so he pushes her to be agentic, to accomplish things—sometimes too much.

Tell me about your father.

I think he still sees me as his little girl. And, I've sort of played into that my whole life, he's very into image. He seems like the father who if I got into Stanford would want to put a Stanford bumper sticker on his car so that everybody would know that his daughter went to Stanford. Umm, he's very…he pushes me to do. In a way my mom doesn't push me enough, and she's always let me make my own decisions. You know, "If you want to quit flute after taking it for five years that's fine," and my dad has always been, "Don't quit. I don't want you to be a quitter," and all this stuff. I think my mom let me give things up too easily but my dad pushed me too hard to stick with things I'd probably be better giving up.

Thus, Heather describes herself in very agentic terms.

Umm, I'm outgoing and I'm very involved in things at school and out-side of school and I think I have a lot of initiative in terms of getting involved. (Pause.) I don't know. When there's something I'm interested in I'm very focused on it, and when there's something that I'm not inter-ested in it's very easy for me to lose motivation…I think I'm really hard on myself in terms of always feeling like I could be doing better than I'm doing and not taking into consideration that maybe for me to get those straight A's I'd have to work my butt off, and I would be a miserable per-son.

Some middle-class girls' descriptions of their fathers sound like the romantic descriptions of their boyfriends that we heard in Chapter Four. They present their fathers as absolutely *wonderful*. Their fathers are idealized in every sense of the word. For example, hearing Kelly's story, one cannot doubt that Benjamin is right about ideal love.

Tell me about your father.

My dad is such a sweetie. Umm, he works a lot, obviously, because he's a doctor, when he's home. He like helped me with my history last night. I had to make up some facts about the Vietnam War going into the debate we had today. Actually it worked too. Nobody even called me on it, but I was willing to say that these facts were straight from the Dr. Richard Kitz, a leading medical practitioner. They weren't made up, but they were projecting figures for deaths, and I mean everybody thought that the Vietnam War was going to be over in six months nobody thought that there would be like all those people killed, so. But he, I swear he knows everything. Like whenever I have like math problems or science prob-lems, I can go to him and if he doesn't know it he can figure it out. And

> he gets all happy after I ask him a question he gets to look up in the ency-
> clopedia or for biology in his old medical books. We do stuff together.
> When I was in public school a lot of times They'd add an extra day to
> vacation for teacher work day and we'd do stuff like go to the zoo and
> now we're thinking, he has his pilot license, and we're gonna go out to
> lunch and fly to Small Sun Bay. We get along great. I used to have prob-
> lems with my mom but it was about stuff like cleaning your room which
> isn't stuff dad really cares about. So, we get along.

As we can see from the above girls' descriptions of their fathers, middle-class fathers encourage their daughters to do and to act. At least at adolescence, middle-class fathers seem to have more ability to recognize their daughters' agency. That is, middle-class fathers encourage their daughters in sports and school, share their interests with them, and acknowledge their abilities and talents. Middle-class girls sustain this relationship of ideal love with their fathers well into adolescence.[170]

Ideal love for the father does not allow middle-class girls sexual subjectivity or desire, however. Middle-class girls feel uncomfortable in their bodies and with their sexuality around their fathers. Many tell stories about their fathers telling them to "cover yourself up" as they reach puberty. Sondra, a middle-class seventeen-year-old, said that her father told her she could not come downstairs in her pajamas anymore and that she had to put a bathrobe on when she got out of bed. Other girls, like Tiffany, a middle-class fifteen-year-old, felt a similar, general discomfort about their bodies and sexuality at puberty.

> I've always basically liked him [my dad]. When I was in seventh and
> eighth grade I was uncomfortable around him. When I was growing up
> I thought (pause), well it's hard to explain. Just because he was my father,
> and I was growing up and having puberty and all that thing, I stayed away
> from him as much as possible.

Apter also finds that adolescent girls "stay away from" their fathers after puberty.[171] Although ideal love allows middle-class girls partial identification with their father and partial agency, it does not facilitate sexual subjectivity and often causes girls to feel ashamed of their bodies, as we saw Chapter Three.

Working-class girls do not identify with their fathers much. Nor, do they sustain a relationship of ideal love from childhood. Their stories about their fathers are not as rich in description or emotion as are middle-class girls' or working-class girls' descriptions of their mothers. Generally, working-class girls depict their fathers as innocuous or authoritarian, and they often compare their fathers to their mothers. For example, they say things like, "He has a bad temper. He's not easy to talk to. He's kind of back in the fifties some-where." Or, "Not quite as close as me and my mom are but, umm, he never yells at me so we get along pretty good." Or, "Umm, just like my mom. I can tell him things, some things I'd rather tell my mom than my father though." Similarly, when I asked Ellen, a working-class sixteen-year-old, if she got along with her father she replied, "I don't really talk to him that much."

Unlike middle-class girls, working-class girls do not indicate any identifica-tion with, recognition from, or ideal love for their fathers. The class differences in identification with father may be due to two things. First, middle-class girls may spend more time doing things with their fathers because some middle-class fathers do more shared parenting and have more leisure time.[172] Where many middle-class girls talked about sharing activities with their fathers, few working-class girls described doing homework, playing sports, or hanging out with them. Second, working-class father's position of authority in the family may keep girls at bay. In Chapter Four we saw that middle-class girls' ideal love for their fathers may be what keeps them from ideal love with peers and thus early sex, while working-class girls embrace it. By adolescence, working-class girls have shifted their ideal love to male peers and boyfriends.

Most girls, working- and middle-class, identify highly and ambivalently with their mothers, particularly in adolescence.[173] At adolescence, girls want both to remain attached to their mothers and to move away from them as in rapprochement. Chodorow suggests that just as girls begin to desire some independence, their pubescent, changing bodies cause them to confront "all the social and psychological issues of being a woman (relations to men, men-struation and feminine reproductive functions, and so forth). In a society in which gender differences are central, this confrontation emphasizes her tie to and identification with her mother."[174]

My research supports these observations. Girls' identifications with their mothers may be positive or negative or ambivalent, yet in any case, when describing their mothers, teenage girls of both classes often describe her in terms of themselves. Kristen, a working-class sixteen-year-old, best expresses girls' ambivalent relationships with their mothers.

> *How would you describe your mother?*
> Right now…is not a good day. But basically, you know, we don't fight. She'll get mad at me and yell at me, but basically I won't yell back at her unless I know I did something, and I'll defend myself. But most of the time she's in a bad mood, and she just takes it out on me. That's real typ-ical of her. But we get along really good. Like mother-daughter stuff. I lie to her all the time, but like she doesn't want to hear it [the truth]. Like I used to tell her about the stuff I did my freshmen year, 'cause I was a hel-

101

> lion, but like she'd just rather not know. She really would, so I lie to her and tell her I'm not going to a party or something like that.

I asked Sondra to tell me about her mother and like many girls she immediately compared her mother to herself.

> Umm (pause), she's a lot like me in good ways and bad ways. She's funny; she's good with people; she tends to be too sarcastic; I think that her experiences have made her kind of negative about men, about relationships and I think that's rubbed off on me and in a way it's good because, because I think I'm more wary, but I think it's also bad because I'm living through her experiences instead of making my own judgments. We get along very well, but the older I get and probably the more similar we get the less we get along. But we definitely go through phases. I mean she's been my best friend probably since I can remember.

Even Jill, a working-class eighteen-year-old, who had a turbulent relationship with her mother, still could not resist comparing her mother and herself. In fact she described her mother, herself, and their relationship when I asked her, "How would you describe your mother?"

> Strict. Very strict. She's from the old country, and that reflects her personality a lot. She's, if you knew me, you could just take me and flip it over. We're totally opposite. She's very, umm, conservative. Likes to go by the book. Really into tradition and not changing anything. Year after year things should be the same. Generations should follow the same things that their parents did. So she's overall conservative and traditional.
> *Do you get along with her?*
> No. We don't get along. If we do speak it is usually in a high tone voice and yelling at each other. But, sometimes if we're not fighting, we talk for maybe fifteen or twenty minutes. Then we just go our separate ways. If she's downstairs, I'm upstairs. If she's home, I'm not. It's just…We don't get along at all. She's black, I'm white. Total opposites.

Girls' identifications with their mothers are all encompassing. From visions of their own futures, feelings about body, to decisions about sex girls identify with their mothers. Many girls said in the course of the interview that they did not want to have a life like their mothers', but then proceeded at the end of the interview to describe a future for themselves, that sounded much like their mothers' lives.

Working-class girls thought about and described their mothers' appearances and bodies, just as they described their own bodies or appearance when telling me about themselves (something boys did not do). For example, when I asked Danielle, a giggly, working-class fifteen-year-old to describe herself (not her appearance) she said, "Well I got long hair and brown eyes. I'm 5'3" and-a-half. I'm fat. [Giggles.] Well, I think I am. Tan, nice, talkative. I don't know what else." When I asked her later in the interview "How would you describe your mother?" she replied by again mixing physical and "personality" traits in her description.

> A bitch. [Laughs.] She's nice. She's a small little lady. She wasn't before, but she lost a lot of weight. She's she's she's...I can use that word can't I? She's a bitch. She's nice sometimes. She like puts on a show for my friends. She'll pretend like I'm doing something wrong and it'll be her. She's just a bitch!

Similarly, but with fewer giggles, Valerie, a working-class sixteen-year-old said,

> Well, we have a good a relationship. Like I tell her everything. Umm, she's just, she's short, pretty, smart, nice. She's just, umm, a fun person to be with.

Working-class adolescent girls, like Danielle and Valerie, are so identified with their mothers that they fear physically becoming their mothers more. They fear that their bodily experiences will be like their mothers', and girls, unfortunately, often do not view their mothers' bodily experiences positively. Mothers' stories about menstrual problems, shame about breasts, and fears about weight become the daughters'. Linda, a working-class fifteen-year-old, expected her menstrual cycle to be like her mothers'.

> Umm, my mother just told me her experience [with menstruation], and she goes through hell with her period. She's like, "I hope that doesn't happen to you." She'd never really told me about it before. I was worried that it would happen to me.

Similarly, Meghan thought all girls might worry about their bodies becoming their mothers' bodies.

> *What other kinds of things do you think girls worry about at puberty?*
> Umm, like if they're gonna, like if their mother has a big chest, and they're gonna worry that they might have one too, and they're gonna feel self-conscious. They wonder if they're gonna be like their mother.

Elaine, a working-class sixteen-year-old, confirmed Meghan's suspicion that girls worry that their bodies will be like their mothers'. Elaine explained, "I diet a lot 'cause my mom has like a lot of trouble with her weight, and it just causes her a lot of problems."

Although the middle-class girls I talked to did not fear that their bodies would be like their mothers, they did look to their mothers' sexual experience when deciding whether or not to have sex. Their mothers' experiences provide the contexts for their own first sexual experiences. I asked Erin, who was fourteen, "How will you know when you are "ready" to have sex?"

> I told my mother and she talked to me about when she was ready she knew that she was just ready. There was no doubt in her mind that she didn't want to have sex. So I think that's like what I'm waiting for. I'm waiting for like not to have any doubts, be one hundred percent sure.

In a different case, Heather was worried that she was late in having sex because she knew her mother had had sex at her age. In worrying she also tried to compare herself to her mother, wondering if her mother was that much more mature than she was.

> When I turned sixteen I started thinking "Wow, this is the age my mother was when she had sex!" You know, she had been so open with me about it, probably thinking that it was a really good thing for her to be open with me about it, and now because I am seventeen and haven't had sex yet, part of me can't help but compare myself to her. Was she that much more mature than I was when she was sixteen?

Middle-class mothers may not be able to offer their daughters sexual subjectivity and the ability to desire. However, unlike working-class mothers, some middle-class mothers—like the above fourteen-year-old's mother—offer girls the ability to say no to sex when they do not desire. This is an important skill for teenage girls. This ability to say no is part of a larger agency that some middle-class mothers provide through identification. A few middle-class girls also said their mothers made them feel good about themselves, encouraged them, and told them to do what they thought was right.[175] "My mother like always tells me I did good, and is encouraging and stuff like that." Or, "Like my mother was always telling me, and now with my sister, that I was beautiful. She kept me from being so self-conscious, and made me feel like I could just be myself." Similarly, Collins finds that African-American mothers teach their daughters independence and survival.[176] Thus, some mothers (see Chapter Six for more on girls and their mothers who are the exceptions) are able to offer their daughters some recognition, some agency and subjectivity, even if they cannot help their daughters construct greater sexual subjectivity.

As we saw in the previous chapters, relationships and identifications with parents play key roles in determining teens experiences throughout puberty and early sexuality. The most important aspect of the parent—adolescent relationship (as in the parent—young child relationship) is recognition. The more recognition adolescents receive for their accomplishments in the world and for their strivings to develop a "grown-up" self, the more agency and sexual subjectivity they will be able to achieve. How adolescent girls and boys feel about their bodies, puberty, and sexuality are all partially built on the recognition or lack of it they receive from parents and others.

"YOU JUST HAVE TO BE TRUE TO YOURSELF"

Girls as Subjects

ALTHOUGH AGENCY and sexual subjectivity are difficult for most girls to achieve, some girls do. Many girls have moments of subjectivity, agency, or sexual subjectivity, and a few girls have built it firmly into their sense of self. Socio-cultural forces do help to shape girls' selves both internally and externally, but they are not completely determining. Girls are able to subvert, reconstruct, and modify these socio-cultural influences, at least occasionally. Research on adolescent girls often depicts them as completely without power and subjectivity, but girls do often speak as subjects and agents.[177] I will not discuss boys much in this chapter, for although they are not complete agents or sexual subjects, the problems of agency and sexual subjectivity are not so great for them, as we have seen in the proceeding chapters. I focus here specifically on what possibilities there might be for girls to feel agentic and sexually subjective.

There are many ways for girls to achieve some agency and sexual subjectivity. Here, I focus on three of these. "Sports/school is my life" agency is a particularly middle-class way of feeling and being active in the world for girls. "Telling off boys" is a type of agency and sexual subjectivity that both working-class girls and middle-class girls practice. It includes a sense of self that refuses to be "walked all over" by boys. Finally, "motherly 'encouragement'" provides some girls with agency and sexual subjectivity. That is, a few mothers give their daughters the confidence to make their own decisions about themselves and about sexuality. None of these types of subjectivity are complete. The girls who can resist boys are still compelled by ideal love, and mothers are better at "encouraging" their daughters to say no to sex than they are at helping them to learn about pleasure. Nonetheless, the girls in each of these categories have been able to establish some agency or sexual subjectivity.

"SPORTS/SCHOOL IS MY LIFE."

Many middle-class girls and a few working-class girls establish themselves as agents and feel like agents in the realms of school and sports. This finding contradicts the AAUW study that sees school as debilitating to girls' self-esteem. Class may make the difference. Many middle-class girls have accomplished a lot in these realms of their lives, as well as in artistic endeavors like music or dance. Heather told me,

108

> I guess I'm confident in school. I'm interested in languages and right now I'm taking French, and Spanish and German. I took Russian a lot of years, I don't remember [how many]. I feel confident with that, especially with Spanish, I've gone and stayed in South America, people like look to me, I get to be everyone's dictionary.

Sharon was artistic, or in her words "really into the arts."

> See I can't be a ballerina 'cause I would've had to have gone away to school and all that kind of stuff and it just takes so much more time than I'm ready to put in right now. Right now I'm doing like plays and stuff with dance so, it's not like professional, it's not like competition and stuff like that but it's mostly umm, for satisfaction and stuff. What was the question?
> *Do you want to do it [ballet] for a career?*
> I don't think I'm gonna. I'd like to maybe do it on the side with something else. I'd just like to keep doing it, but I don't know if I want to go into it for a career. I also paint and do art and stuff like that.

Girls who played sports seriously also had a committment to something that made them feel proud. It also made them less susceptible to making their boyfriends the center of their lives because they were "so busy with like other stuff." Participating in sports may be one way (although somewhat removed from sexuality) for girls to connect body, agency and self. Madeleine Blais' account of the Amherst High School girls' basketball team, *In These Girls, Hope is a Muscle*, demonstrates that through a passionate commitment to a team sport, girls learn to expect the best of themselves and each other.[178] They learn confidence in themselves and in their bodies. They feel agentic, and in many cases, they are recognized by others for their talents and commitments. They also become able to recognize each other and learn to admire and respect other each other. Lucia, one the youngest players on the team Blais writes about, wrote the following in her journal:

> Today I realized how much I love basketball. We lost the Western Mass semifinals to Hamp. The game was a blur. All I remember was how we were in constant struggle to come back. We started off well, but after the refs gave Hamp a boost, they ran with the ball. No one played excep-tionally well besides Jamila, who was the high scorer with thirty points. Jenny wasn't having a good night and the forwards couldn't get the ball to sink either. I felt as if everything that the team had worked for so long just left our grasp.
>
> It's not fair. It's not fair. The team has some of the finest athletes in the world, not to mention the most funny, smart, beautiful, incredibly awe-some people ever to walk the earth. Just seeing anyone on the team makes my day. Jamila has got to be the sweetest person. She is funny, beautiful, amazingly athletic, and to top that off she is nice to everyone. Jenny is the one person who I respect and love the most. She seems to know every-thing and whenever she speaks to me I'm speechless because I look up to her so much. I love it when she slaps my hand, or hugs me. It makes me feel like I'm worth something.

109

Such admiration and respect of one teenage girl for another is rare. Blais seems to suggest that girls' sports can facilitate these feelings, as well as agency and self-esteem.

Thus, in these straightforward ways that revolve around school, sports, and other talents, girls describe themselves as actors, doers, and agents. Middle-class girls take pride in their talents and accomplishments in these realms, and as we have seen in previous chapters, middle-class parents recognize girls' accom-plishments in these activities more than working-class parents do. For some middle-class girls, school, school activities (student council, "lend-a-hand," the big-sister program), sports or other special talents (like art or music) make them feel agentic in part of their life. However, little of this acting involves girls' bodies, particularly their sexual bodies, and even girls who were involved in sports or dance sometimes said that their bodies were not appropriately feminine, were the wrong shape, or the wrong size.

"TELLING OFF BOYS…"

Two girls, Kristen (sixteen, working-class) and Kelly (seventeen, middle-class), both late developers, presented a form of agency and sexual subjectivity that was built on "not taking any shit from guys." This type of agency had an element of feminism in it that girls combined with stories about "I learned the hard way." These girls simultaneously "bad mouthed" all men and told stories about ideal love. However, it is clear from their narratives that they derived a sense of strength from resisting (many) boys' sexual advances and claiming that they would not be led astray by boys.

Kristen described herself as agentic and active, as someone who made her opinion known and who stuck by her decisions. She clearly was not subjected to the "tyranny of nice and kind."

[I'm] stubborn about things, and like…I don't know. I'm loud a lot. Actually too loud a lot. I always have to say something. I always have to get my word in. Always. I always have to say what I think…I was kind of a little shit when I was a kid. I used to like play jokes on people. I was always like the leader of everything and kind of bossy and control, always have to be in control. I used to want to be a housewife when I was ten. Sit around the house and have kids. Well I still want to have kids but I want to have a job, you know.

When I asked her if she had changed her mind about being a housewife and having kids, her sense of resisting boys and being an independent woman (her version of feminism) kicked in.

Why do you think that changed?
Ummm. Just because, I don't know…I'm a wicked feminist. I like I kill [meaning talk bad about] men all the time. I just basically, like when I started dating I just basically woke up.
What about dating did that?
Men are all pigs! No like, I just wicked like consider men like the weather. Like they're never dependable, seasonal, they change all the time. I umm, temporary. I just don't want to be dependent on a man and if I was a housewife I would be.

Kristen's mother is a single mother who raised Kristen and her sister on her own. Although she and her mother did not get along, Kristen had tremendous respect for her mother because of her hard work and self-respect. "She's awesome! I mean my father was a jerk and she left him. And it's the best thing that ever happened to her and she like totally raised me and my sister and she did so much for us, but she's just tired of having kids now." It seems that part of her evaluation of men and their dependability came from an understanding of her mother's life.

When I asked Kristen if there was a goal that she had achieved or something that she was proud of, she answered,

> Um, well, I wasn't gonna have sex until I was at least sixteen, and I had to be in love and all that stuff and when all my friends were all out freshmen year getting laid by every guy, I didn't.
> *How did you achieve that goal? Was it hard?*
> It was wicked hard. Wicked hard. I had to like...well I used to date all the guys but, like, they would never get anything so they would never last that long because the guys I dated were all jerks, seniors guys who wanted to get high, and stoned, and drunk and get laid or...I wasn't that little typical freshmen girl so...I'm just not gonna let guys walk all over me.

When I asked Kristen what advice she would give to other girls about dating and sex, she replied,

111

> [I'd tell them] to make more friends than boyfriends. Because they come and go, and, just basically, don't give anybody your virginity. Don't. It takes so much time to know [if it's right], you know. Freshmen year don't get drunk and make out with all the little boys. Umm, just totally not to...make more friends than boyfriends. Don't ever ever choose a boyfriend over a friend. A friend's always going to be there for you. Don't let a guy come between and stuff like that.

Kelly, from a middle-class family where her mom no longer works, says similar things. She did not want to "put up with" boys treating her badly and felt that she did not have to, that there were "plenty of fish in the sea" and she would "find one that is decent and not like a typical high school guy."

> I went out with this one guy for another two months, last year who was, I mean, it was, he was nice, but he didn't, I mean, the point for him of us going out was for him to eventually sleep with me. And this was not my point. And so we finally broke up after he said, you know, "I'm sorry but I really want to be in a relationship where I have sex with somebody," he

did not say this nearly as eloquently. Basic high school jerk, right? I said "I'm sorry but that's not really gonna happen with me unless I feel like I really love the person and they love me back." And he was like "Okay, it's not gonna work out," and the next three times I saw him he was just completely drunk and like really saying awful things about me.

And there was like this other jerk that I went out with for another two months. And he was, I finally just got sick of him, and I don't understand how I went out with him for that long. He was like not...well he only called when he felt like it or felt like he had the time, or he'd like come over by surprise when he had like nothing better to do. And so, so finally, I just like, I called him up and I had left a shirt and I go "I need my shirt 'cause a friend of mine has to borrow it," so he came over and brought me the shirt and like tried to give me a hug and I just screamed at him, I mean he must have been so confused, it came so completely out of the blue. But I wasn't gonna take anything like that from him.

Both of these girls felt like they had rights that were worth sticking up for. They both disparaged boys, especially boys they dated a lot. However, their resistance to boys and their critiques of dating did not replace feelings of and wishes for ideal love. When I asked Kristen, who did not want to be dependent on a man, what she daydreamed about, she said, "Getting married. All the time. I can't wait. I'm gonna wait, so that's something." When I asked her what she really wanted to accomplish in her life she revealed the tension she felt between feelings about ideal love and feelings about what she calls "feminism."[179] "I want to get married. That sounds so corny, but I'm such a feminist, I want women to be that, but I want to get married, I don't want to be an old lady." Thus, although some girls express agency and sexual subjectivity by resisting boys and standing up for themselves and girls in general, they are not able banish all feelings of ideal love that lead girls to follow boys.

"MOTHERLY 'ENCOURAGEMENT.'"

The two girls in my sample who exhibited the most agency and some sexual subjectivity were Samantha (sixteen) and Erin (fourteen). They were both attending the predominantly working-class public high school, but both had parents who were more educated than most working-class teens' parents. Both said their parents had wanted to send them to private school but could not afford it, and in this way they are also different from the (upper) middle-class teens I interviewed. Both Samantha and Erin seem to derive their agency and strong sense of self from their mothers. Here I describe their general similarities and how they were different from the other girls in the sample. Then below I describe each of them in more detail.

Samantha and Erin were both involved in school activities—student council, peer counseling, etc. Samantha also played tennis and field hockey, and while Erin described herself as "not athletic," she was a dedicated dancer. While most girls who played sports said they did because "it's fun" or "for exercise" or "for something to do," Samantha said she played sports because "I like to win," and Erin said she danced because "I like to perform." Winning and performing are active, agentic descriptions of why they participated in sports and dance.

Samantha and Erin were both more comfortable with their bodies than the other girls I talked to. For example, each was excited about getting her first period, and neither complained about it. Both used tampons without negative comments and from the beginning of their periods. Both had consciously and thoughtfully decided not to have sex at this time in their lives.

All of the above similarities inform and evidence the agency and sexual subjectivity these girls were able to construct and maintain, but two other things they had in common seem especially key to their developing a confidence in and a claim to their body and sexuality. Each had a confident sense of knowing and doing for oneself and a strong, open relationship with a mother who recognized her daughter's self, agency, and abilities. These two factors are connected. The mother-daughter relationships I describe below, especially Erin's, facilitated each girl's development of this confident sense of self.

SAMANTHA.

Samantha was one of the first girls I interviewed, and she volunteered to do so because as class treasurer she was anxious for her class—the Juniors—to earn the donation I had promised to the classes who participated. At the beginning of our conversation she cuddled up in her big, oversized sweatshirt with her school's name on it. We began by talking about what she thought she was like when she was 10 years old. Samantha told me, contrary to Gilligan's and Hancock's romanticized views of childhood,[180] that she liked herself better now than when she was ten. "Just cause like…Just 'cause I know more. I guess like I know more about what annoys me that I do myself. Back then I'd just do it. I know myself better now."

Samantha said that it was her mother who had "given" her this self. She referred often to her mother's "motherly encouragement," and how it had helped her to "kinda know myself better, and know what I should do and stuff."

Knowing herself was a predominant theme throughout our conversation. For example, Samantha talked at length about a hard decision she had to make when she decided not to tell her mother that she was going to a party. Her mother did not want her to go because she was afraid that Samantha could get caught up in the drinking and drugs that were going on, even though

Samantha had assured her that she would never do that. She explained to me that she knew herself and expressed that this was a knowing that she had complete confidence in—enough confidence, even, to make a decision that went against her mother's wishes. Samantha told the story this way,

> My mother won't let me go to parties, umm, unless there's a parent there. Probably, that's like one of my things that, I know myself and I know what I would and wouldn't do, and she knows it too, but its her like doing her safe parent thing.
> *She knows you wouldn't do what?*
> She knows like I wouldn't just go crazy, and get totally drunk, and do drugs or something and go off and kill someone's house and start driving around afterwards, drive off the road or drive into somebody else or something, but…But she still says no, so…I'm like 'I'm going out' which surprises me that she's just like, 'Oh, okay.' And we'll like go to a party, but we're not like, we don't do anything, because I know I won't do it so, so I won't…It's not like I lied to her but…It's like I didn't tell her and I know she doesn't want me to do it but…I know what I do and I know what's right and wrong, so I just figure that as long as I do what I know I can and should that it's not that bad…

Samantha's self-knowledge gave her confidence to act against her mother's wishes. It also gave her confidence in relationships with boys. She said that one of the things that made her scared about sex was being embarrassed if she asked a boy to use a condom and he would not, because then she would have to say no to sex and that would be awkward. But she asserts that in spite of the embarrassment she would say no, because she knows herself.

> I'd be like scared if I like didn't want to and someone else did and if I was like, if I had the condom I got in school, and they were like, "I'm not gonna use that" then I'd have to be like…I'd probably look like a dork, but I'd be like "Well, I'm sorry." Like I'd do it, I'd say no because I'd know that's what I wanted to do, but I wouldn't want to 'cause I'd feel, not embarrassed 'cause I'd know that I wanted to do it, but I'd just feel stupid. It'd be hard. Just 'cause I'd be like the one who'd say no. But I'd do it.

Samantha attributes this knowing what she wants to do about sex from talking to her mother about sex since she was very young. She says that her mother's easy going attitude about it, that it was "not a big deal" made talking and knowing about sex easier. She explains,

> She doesn't do the sit-down and have-a-talk thing, but our family is just like, we just have books and stuff, and not like here read this…They've [the books have] just always been around. Just like when I got to school [and took health education] I was just like "Yeah, okay, I already know this."
> *How old were you when they first started talking to you about it?*
> Forever. Just like when we were really little…It was just always like there, so it was never a big deal.

Samantha also said that starting her period was not a big deal. She said she was happy "especially 'cause I was so late." She was fourteen. She said that her mother "didn't say anything. She was just like 'Oh, okay, here.' Before she was just like 'Oh, we have stuff in the closet if you ever need it.' I'm just like 'okay.'" Samantha goes on to say that because her mother did not make a big deal out of it "I didn't care." She also says, in contrast to most of the girls I talked to,

> I don't mind having it now. I just get it and it's like [no big deal—she shrugs her shoulders]. I don't get sick or anything. My friends all get sick and they have to go home. They take medication and stuff. I don't understand it and because then they try to tell me and stuff and I'm just like I don't have that…?

Brooks-Gunn and Ruble explain Samantha's experience. They find a correlation between physical symptoms and social experience of puberty. That is, the more information a girl had about menstruation prior to menarche and the better the information, then the fewer physical menstrual problems, like cramps, she experienced.[181]

ERIN AND HER MOTHER.

Erin, like Samantha, expressed a confidence in herself and her decisions that was not exhibited by many of the other girls. She was relaxed throughout the interview and only exhibited a little nervousness by pushing her long, straight, brown hair out of her eyes and behind her ears every few minutes. She was extremely articulate and mature for fourteen years old and much of our conversation was like talking to a friend.

As we began the interview, I asked her to describe herself. Erin said that as she had gotten older she had learned to be "outgoing," "to express myself freely," and "to speak my mind." Many of the girls I interviewed had a difficult time answering questions like "What are you afraid of?" "What are you confident about?" "What things come easy for you?" etc. Erin answered these clearly and easily. For example, when asked what she was afraid of she replied,

Mmmmm. I would've liked to do like sports and stuff like, but sometimes
I'm with my friends, and they play softball and stuff, softball and soccer
and things like that you know, I would if I had started earlier [younger],
you know, but I'm so afraid of being bad at it. That's like my fear, to be
embarrassed about it and stuff like that. I like to do things that I know
I'm good at. Maybe that's what I don't like about myself that like, I like
to do new things if I know that it's not like, that somebody else is already
really, really a lot better at it than me or if it's like a competition, kind of
like a team sport, like something depends on me and maybe you let
somebody down or something.

Erin used her self-knowledge in deciding not to have sex with her
boyfriend. She had been dating a boy a year older than she for three months.
She described their relationship with the comment "I think we get along real
good." He wanted them to have sex, but she was not ready, and said that she
had tried to communicate that to him.

He says "You haven't done it yet, you don't know why I want to have
sex." Because, so I just said…"Are you thinking about if I don't have sex
with you, I don't love you?" and he goes "Bingo!" And I said, "Well, that's
not it at all. I knew you would say that but it's not." So I was just trying
to make him understand. I hope he does because I'm not ready yet.
How will you know when you're ready? What does being ready mean?
Well, I told my mother and she talked to me about when she was ready
she knew that she was ready. There was no doubt in her mind that she
wanted to have sex. So I think that's like what I'm waiting for. I'm waiting for like not to have any doubts, to be one hundred percent sure. You
just have to be true to yourself.

A little later in the interview I asked her what advice she would give to a
younger girl about sex.

…Like waiting until you're really ready and it's you that counts and it's
you that's making the decision and I mean maybe you're not gonna be
with this boyfriend for the rest of your life so if you do it just to satisfy
him and like you don't see him any more then what's left for you? I mean
you haven't satisfied yourself and it's like you're left with nothing so…and
knowing all the facts. I think that's real important and they can make their
own decisions based on real strong, like knowing the consequences and
things like that.

Erin, only fourteen years old, expresses sexual subjectivity in these passages from our interview. The idea of doing for oneself, of satisfying oneself, of having something left for the self, are all unusual concepts in teen girls' narratives.

As one may notice from Erin's discussion above, her mother played a significant part in her development of her sense of self and of her sexual subjectivity. Throughout our conversation, Erin talked both about herself and about her mother. When I asked Erin what she thought about condoms being made available to students in the high school, she responded, "I am for that because, ummm, my mother is too, but I guess that's beside the point." Then she went on to tell me why she *and* her mother thought it was a good idea.

When I asked her about starting her period, getting her first bra, and shaving, all her answers were a mix of how she felt and how her mother felt and responded. When I asked her how she felt after she shaved the first time she said she felt like her mother. Although several other girls also talked specifically about shaving as something that made them feel grown up and like their mothers, none of them did it so consistently or positively as did Samantha and especially Erin. When I asked Erin to describe her mother, she said,

> My mother. Umm. She's, I'm very much like her. And, like, she's like, like in the past couple of years, like when I was younger you know, I just was more like not into myself. [Meaning, I didn't know myself.] And she's helped me become that kind of person and since I have, like I've become…like she always speaks her mind wherever she wants…She's just real set in what she thinks and things like that, and she'll argue it and so she's helped me become, like that kind of person.
>
> Since I have, we get along real good and I can talk to her about everything. She understands and she trusts like my judgment so that like gives me confidence to make the right decisions, and she leads with like education 'cause she's also in the school system. So she's like into education to help you make the right decision. It's just better than knowing nothing at all.

Thus, Erin claims that her mother has helped her to become the person she now understands herself to be. Similarly, Apter finds that daughters "individuate" and become adults not in separating from mother but through connection with her.[182] However, Apter, like Chodorow sees enormous conflict resulting from a daughter's attempt to individuate while maintaining connection with her mother.[183] While Samantha's description of her relationship with her mother exhibited some of this conflict, Erin's did not. Perhaps, since she was only fourteen, it was yet to come.

117

Erin attributes her confidence in her body, her appearance, and as we saw above, her decision not to have sex, to her mother. She says that her mother usually reacted positively to the many rites of passage of puberty. Erin says that she was excited about developing breasts and adds, "My mom too, like to buy me my first bra or something." Erin started her first period at her best friend's house, and after telling her best friend, she called her mom who said "Oh, that's great." She goes on to say, "I used pads for like a week and then I started using tampons, 'cause pads are like the most uncomfortable thing, and like my mom showed me how to put a tampon in, so it was just like I used that ever since, and I just can't use pads now."

This is an unusual account in the context of the other interviews. Many girls did not use tampons until well "used to" menstruating. Most girls learned about tampons from trial and error or occasionally from an older sister or a friend. Samantha's mother also encouraged her to use tampons (although did not actually show her how to use them), and Samantha used tampons from menarche. Most mothers, however, seemed to have a fear of their daughters using tampons,[184] or at least that is the message most daughters received from their mothers. Erin was the only one who said that her mother actually taught her how to use them.

Erin's mother was also able to provide Erin with a confidence about her appearance. As we have seen, when I asked most girls if they liked the way they looked the answer was either no or an ambiguous, qualified yes. Many girls were genuinely dissatisfied, depressed, or even disgusted with their appearance. Erin and Samantha made the most positive comments about their bodies to me. When I asked Erin if she liked the way that she looked she said, "Yeah, I do. I do sometimes. I don't like ever say I hate myself or I hate the way that I look, but sometimes I'll say, 'I just can't stand my hair today,' or something like that. I think everybody does that." Then when I asked her if she thought others found her attractive, she said yes. In explaining why she was confident about her appearance she says, "My mother tells me, my mother says I look nice and stuff...it makes me feel better about myself and encourages me and stuff." She says her mother does the same for her sister who is now developing breasts and is self-conscious about it. "I think like my mother is always telling her she's so beautiful and things like that and it just makes her feel like less, like it's not like bad, even though she does look older." This is very similar to Erin's comment's above about how her mother talked to her about how she decided to have sex. Again, it seems her mother is providing her with the confidence in herself and her body. Whereas fathers often sexualize daughters as heterosexual objects, mothers can help daughters to become heterosexual subjects.[185]

Finally, Erin was one of the few girls in the sample who could say more about what she wanted for her future than the standard "I want to go to college/or get a job/get married/have kids/be happy." Few girls gave more specifics to this life track, and even fewer still could envision another track. Again, Erin envisions something different seemingly because she had talked to her mother about her mother's own life.

First, Erin had a picture in her mind of what college would be like, whereas most girls could only say they wanted to go or perhaps what they wanted to major in. It seemed as if her mother painted some of this picture. Erin described college,

> Umm, I think it's gonna be great. I think it's gonna be so much fun, like on my own and stuff. Probably live in a dorm or maybe off campus, with like some friends, like other girls, umm, who go to the same college and stuff, and oh just really cool and like hanging out and stuff...(laughs) I don't think about the work when you go to college and stuff.

Then, talking more explicitly about her mother, she tells me what she wants to do with the rest of her life after college.

> I definitely, when I get out of college, well this is what I say to myself...I want to like travel around the world. I don't want to get married right away. My mother got married when she was like twenty-one and I think that's so young, even if she waited until she was like twenty-eight to have me...She said she would have liked to travel and when she talked to me about it I just think that sounded so great to just like see the world so that you're not like tied down with somebody else. If you meet somebody, you know, things could happen, you know when you meet somebody. But I probably picture myself just living...I don't know what kind of job I'll have. Something kind of artsy, kind of laid back.

119

Erin's mother provided her with a different vision of her own life. Some of the girls whom I spoke with said they absolutely did not want to be like their mothers when I asked them early in the interview to describe her, yet when I asked about their future at the end of the interview, they described lives that sounded very much like their mothers' lives, except that they often included "Be happy," which they thought their mothers were not. Erin's mother told her daughter the dream, the possibilities that she had given up, and although she still feared repeating her mother's life ("Things could happen"), this allowed Erin to see other possibilities for herself.

Both Samantha and Erin developed agency and some sexual subjectivity (the sense that they had a right to their bodies, although little sense that they could take pleasure in their bodies) in relationship to their mothers. I am not suggesting that it is mothers' fault that all girls do not have sexual subjectivity. Rather, that by looking at mothers who are able to facilitate sexual subjectivity in their daughters, we might learn how women can begin to recognize teenage girls' sexuality in a positive way, one that both affirms the pleasure and acknowledges the danger of being a (hetero) sexually active teenage girl.

Thus, all girls are not determined by the social and cultural forces that restrict women's agency and sexuality. All girls do not have equal opportunities or abilities to work against these social and cultural pressures, but many are able to construct subjectivity in some realms of their lives. Some girls are even able to establish significant amounts of agency or sexual subjectivity. Middle-class girls can often construct agency from their accomplishments in sports and school. They receive recognition for these accomplishments from their peers, teachers, and parents that make them feel like they can act and do meaningful things in these realms. Sports and school do not directly facilitate the construction of sexual subjectivity (although feeling agentic in other realms may help girls to feel sexually agentic), but rather girls who are involved in sports and school often put off first sex longer than other girls do, and this keeps them from quickly losing sexual subjectivity. Mothers seem to be able to be the vehicle for facilitating some development of sexual subjectivity (and agency) in teenage girls.

"HOW GUYS APPROACH YOU AND WHAT YOUR CHOICES ARE"

Looking for Solutions

WHY DOES girls' self-esteem drop so much more than boys' does at adolescence? Broadly, puberty and first sexual experiences affect girls and boys quite differently. More specifically girls' self-esteem drops because girls learn cultural meanings about gender, particularly negative discourses about women's bodies and female sexuality, that cause them to feel devalued. Girls learn as they develop through puberty that they are headed toward an adult female sexuality that is derogated. Thus, they often feel fat, dirty, ugly, objectified or ashamed of their bodies, a fundamental part of the self. Similarly, girls' first sexual experiences tend to leave them feeling confused, unagentic, unpleasured, and unsure of themselves, their decisions, and their bodies. These feelings all take a toll on girls' self-worth. Boys are also affected by puberty and first sex, yet not as negatively as girls are. In particular, boys often feel uncertain about their bodies' changes. This may account for the smaller drop in boys' self-esteem. However, boys' first sexual experiences often serve to bolster their agency, masculinity, and self-worth.

So what can we do about this drop in girls' self-esteem? What would make puberty and first sexual experiences easier, even pleasurable for girls? Although the problem I describe manifests itself psychologically, a solution is not likely to be found at the individual or psychological level because the cause of this problem is rooted in gendered meanings and social interactions. Thus, we must look for social and cultural solutions to the problem of adolescent girls' lower self-esteem. We must change the cultural discourses about gender and sexuality. However, short of widespread change in these cultural meanings, changes in sex education and implementation of gender education would improve girls' (and boys') self-esteem and ease their transitions from childhood to adulthood.

SEX EDUCATION.

Schools must improve sex education. "Sex ed." or "health ed." now often starts in the primary grades and includes pubertal education as well as sex and reproductive education (and often a variety of other topics under the guise of health—smoking, nutrition, car safety, and etc.). Changes in both the pubertal and sex curriculum might correct or mute some of the problems girls and boys face in these areas.

Girls would benefit more from pubertal education, whether delivered by parents or schools, if the information they received was less clinical and biological and more subjective and experiential. As we saw in Chapter Three, many girls who have information on menarche, still do not know when they see the blood from their bodies that they have begun menstruating. Girls appear to need more concrete, experiential descriptions of what menarche and menstruating will be like. Similarly, boys may need more information in general about their pubertal changes, since these changes are often so subtle or undiscussed that boys tend to feel uneasy because they do not know if what they are experiencing is, for example, voice change or a sore throat, if it is a wet dream or they have "wet the bed."

Also, since many adolescents seemed to learn much about puberty from slightly older peers, sisters, brothers, and cousins, pubertal education at school might work better if it were not age-graded. Adults, as the teens in my sample suggest, often link discussions of puberty with discussions of gender roles or female sexuality; teenagers did not do this when I asked them what they would tell a younger child about puberty. Their advice was often more grounded and came from experience. They made suggestions like "Be sure you have a pad with you, but just kind of hide it or some people would like tease you about it." Or, "Don't worry about it if it's [the blood] kinda brown, but ask your mom if you do." A pubertal education program comprised of age-mixed groups might let younger adolescents hear about and learn from the experience of older adolescents in a structured setting. Information about puberty might also be transmitted better between children and adolescents than from adults to adolescents.

Sex education is more complicated than pubertal education, and there is much political debate about it, all of which cannot be addressed here. However, many feminist writers and theorists suggest that sex education is not working for girls.[186] Fine's data from studying sex education in New York City, suggests that public school sex education promotes a discourse of female sexual victimization, privileges married heterosexuality over all other sexual practices, and suppresses any discourse about female sexual desire and plea-sure.[187] The lack of discussion about female desire in sex education courses is also particularly disturbing and problematic.[188] Kendra criticized the way women's desire was portrayed to her,

> Women are taught really confusing messages about their own sexuality, and we're supposed to be either this wild sex symbol, like crazy body and man's wildest fantasy or else like completely rigid and like have the guy like show us our sexual body or something...I know girls who really liked a guy and really liked what they were doing and would've felt com-fortable doing what they were doing, except they had all these messages in their head and like, "You should be saying no more," and "You should be hard to get," which is ridiculous.

123

Thompson suggests that sex education based on the slogan, "Just Say 'Not Until I Know I Want You,'" would do more for girls than "Just Say No" or the more liberal "Just Say Not Now." Girls need to be taught about sexual desire and to gain a sense of entitlement to it. They must be taught by parents, peers, or schools that girls should have sex when they desire it both emotionally and physically. "Being ready" needs to be defined as a physical as well as an emo-tional or adult state. Girls will know they are ready, according to Thompson, if they answer "yes" to most of the following questions.

> Do you get wet when you have a romantic or sexual dream? When you think about kissing or petting? Do your genitals become warm or feel pleasure? Do you know where your clitoris (joy button, little man in a boat) is? Have you touched it? Excited it?...Do you have an idea of what an orgasm is? Have you visualized or imagined what it will be like to be naked with someone? To kiss or pet without clothes on? Have you tried it?..."[189]

Sex education that taught girls to ask these questions would help girls to discover a "desire of one's own."

Feminists are not the only one's critiquing sex education, however. When interviewing, I found teenage girls, much more than boys, very eager to talk about sex education classes and to both commend and critique them. Although I suspect educators think they are treating boys and girls fairly by holding coed sex education classes, several of the girls in my study said their classes would be much better if the girls and boys were not in the same classroom together. For example, Michelle said, "...You know they started having boys and girls together in the class and that's even worse...the guys and girls together! The guys will just sit there and make jokes." Meghan similarly commented,

> It's kind of uncomfortable sometimes when they teach about it. We saw
> movies and stuff about sexual abuse and all that.
> *Was it boys and girls together?*
> Yeah, yup. I think it'd be better to have it separate. It'd be easier. 'Cause
> the girls can relate to each other and stuff and the boys can just relate to
> it. I think it'd be easier.

Other girls suggested that if teachers talked more about relationships, emotions, and social relations and less about physiology and internal organs, then they would have learned more useful material in their courses. Similarly, Ward and Taylor find in their work with six different ethnic groups of teens whom they spoke to in focus groups "a desire to know more about relationships and how to negotiate them." Girls from all six groups—Vietnamese, Portuguese, Black, White, Haitian, and Hispanic—expressed this desire.[190] Among the girls in my study, Andrea said she was tired of hearing about birth control and wanted to know more about relationships, and Kristen thought that girls need to know about the "emotional steps" one must go through before having sex.

> *What would you teach in a sex education course?*
> Ummm? What are the right circumstances and wrong circumstances to
> have sexual intercourse. That might just be one's morals. But you should-
> n't just jump into bed with someone you meet who is really attractive.
> But umm, I think they should learn about what emotional steps they
> should go through to see if they're prepared to have sexual intercourse.
> And tell them that they have to make their own decisions; parents can't
> make those decisions for them. They're gonna have to go through those
> steps themselves, and I think they should be taught what those steps are.

Tracy wished that she could have learned "how boys really are" in her sex education class.

> They just taught, they didn't really teach, well, yeah, they taught sex. Like VD and stuff like that. It was really pretty good 'cause the teacher was good, but made it better? Maybe they could've stressed more, talked about relationships or something. 'Cause when I [started] high school I had no—I don't know what they could teach—but I had no clue of what boys were like, you know, how they are! I don't know…

Similarly, when I asked Diana what she would tell a younger girl about sex she said that she "would like tell them what to expect. You know, how guys would approach you. What your choices are." I asked her, "What do you mean? What kinds of things would you tell them to expect from boys?" She replied,

> How they'll approach you. Like take you out on a date and some of them feel like you owe them sexual favors because they took you out. And sometimes they say "Hey, want to do this?" And sometimes you want to do it 'cause you want to be popular, but I guess it all depends on what your morals are and what your background is, but I guess just to let them know that they do have a choice. They're not obligated to do anything you know. Stuff like that.

125

We can learn from listening to the voices of these girls and to their suggestions, and again, I suggest that sex education in mixed-age groups might also be useful to girls, since many had strong opinions on what they thought younger girls should know given their own experiences. Much useful advice and information might come from older girls' experiences, and younger girls might be more apt to listen to the voice of a peer than of an adult teacher. These suggestions might also be useful for bettering boys' sex education as well. Although boys did not have as strong opinions about sex education as girls did, a few boys did suggest that they had learned from older peers. For example, Brent said that he was only going to have sex with a girl whom he really liked because many of his friends had had one night stands and regretted it. Thus, boys would also learn from both the positive and negative sexual experiences of their peers as well. Finally, my data suggest that adolescents may need gender education as much as they need sex education, or at least, they need sex education in the context of gender education

GENDER EDUCATION FOR BOYS AND GIRLS.

Thorne describes childhood as "a period in which gender relations are relatively egalitarian" because "boys of elementary school age lack major sources of adult male privilege, such as access to greater income and material resources, control of political and other forms of public power and the legal and labor entitlements of husbands and wives."[191] Adolescent boys, although still without all the privilege of adult men, begin to have more access to material and public power. For example, several working-class girls complained that their brothers had access to cars that they did not. Cars are a powerful means of freedom and privilege when one is a teenager. Particularly in dating and partying, those with cars have more choice over where to go, what to do, and when to leave. Teenage boys also begin to control public space. The streets outside the high school and the hallways inside are where many girls are objectified or taunted. Particularly in the working-class school, I often heard boys call girls names, comment on their appearances and the like. Also, Thorne omits any discussion of psychological and discursive power. By adolescence, many boys begin to develop more personal and cultural agency than many girls. Boys' growing knowledge of misogynist discourses (i.e. that girls and women's bodies are dirty), and access to gendered cultural narratives that they know how to use (for example, "If you love me, you will") are also sources of power. Adolescence is not as egalitarian as Thorne finds childhood to be, and this inequality affects teens' experiences of puberty and especially sex.

However, both parents and schools teach both boys and girls about sex with little reference to this unequal social context.

> When the body is the tangible ground of sexual discourse, the focus is usually on the instruction of anatomy, physiology, and sexual infections and diseases. Absent is discussion of the social body, with its cultural differences in feelings, meanings and daily experiences.[192]

Parents, particularly fathers, may warn girls about boys, but these warnings do little to help girls understand the structural nature of gender inequality and instead further the "boys against the girls" attitude that many hold from childhood. Feminism and sociology would suggest that teens must learn more than anatomy, "Just Say No" or "Beware of Boys" in sex education courses. The concept of sex education must be broader—and not simply to include issues of car safety as some health courses do now—but to include a discussion of the social and cultural constructions of things like marriage, contraception, abortion, gay and lesbian issues, child care, sexual abuse, other reproductive rights, rape, pornography, and sex education itself.[193] Thus, as much as adolescents need sex education they need gender education, or at the very least, sex education that pays attention to the gender unequal context in which "natural" sexuality takes place.

Adolescent girls and boys must both learn about socially structured gender inequalities and how they affect their lives. Simple exercises like teaching teens to critique beauty standards portrayed in fashion magazines might help teenage girls to feel less like physical failures and help teenage boys to be less judgmental. An awareness of the socially constructed nature of beauty will not end girls' physical critiques of themselves, but it might, over time, tone down the intensity or at least give girls another way of thinking about beauty—a way that does not construct them as personal failures.

Finally, adolescent girls' loss of self-esteem, must be seen as a consequence of gender oppression in our society at large. Teens should be made aware of this inequality, but more importantly large scale social change needs to take place in order to fully protect the selves of future generations of adolescent girls.

MOVING TOWARD ADULTHOOD.

If we pay attention to what teens have to say about their lives and about the issues of sex, gender, and self-esteem, we might shed light on the adult versions of these same problems. Agency and sexual subjectivity for most girls may reach its lowest point at mid-adolescence. Girls at about eighteen years old began to express somewhat more sexual subjectivity. Many claimed to have arrived at this by "learning the hard way." Some of these girls also said they now, finally, found sex physically pleasurable. However, it seems that for many women this loss of sexual subjectivity at adolescence extends into adulthood. We know from feminist and sociological research that gender inequality in sexual encounters continues to be a problem in adulthood.[194] Adolescence is where these problems in women's sexual subjectivity often originate, and thus, the feminist attention to adolescence needs to begin to explore further the bodily and sexual aspects of adolescence and how it shapes adult women's sexuality and agency.

METHODOLOGICAL APPENDIX

SAMPLE.

MY SAMPLE consists of students from three high schools—one working-class, public high school and two upper-middle-class, private high schools. In the public school, I chose a random sample of sixty students, thirty boys and thirty girls. They were invited to an assembly where I explained the interview project and asked them to participate. Eight students did not attend the assembly due to absence, exams, or having transferred from the school. Twelve said they did not want to participate. Ten either did not return (the rather formidable) consent forms or did not appear for interviews even when rescheduled. The remaining thirty returned consent forms and were interviewed. I interviewed all the students for an hour or more in a private room at school. In each of the private schools I asked for student volunteers through teachers and principals. In the first private school I interviewed students both at school and in neighboring coffee shops. In the second private school I interviewed students for an hour or more in a private room at the school.

Interviewing at school was not a problem and probably enhanced participation. School is the site where adolescents talk most about sex and live their social lives. This talk goes on constantly between classes in hallways, in the cafeteria, outside of school before the first bell, in bathrooms at school, and in notes passed in classes. Teens are certainly more comfortable talking about sex at school than they are at home with parents possibly nearby and on their parents' "turf." Not one student expressed reservations or hesitation about being interviewed in a private room at school.

I interviewed twenty-three boys and thirty-two girls. The new feminist interest in adolescent girls[195] has generated almost no research comparing them to boys, and there is little other sociological or psychological research that does this either. How do Brown and Gilligan know that it is being a girl that causes one to "silence" what one knows, if they have not interviewed boys as well. Perhaps all children do this at adolescence. Similarly, how does Tolman know which experiences of sex are caused by one's gender (and which caused by simply being an adolescent) if she does not also examine boys' experiences of sex? Thus, interviewing both boys and girls was crucial to this project.

The mean age of the students whom I interviewed was sixteen years old. The boys were slightly below that mean and the girls slightly above it. I coded interviewees' socioeconomic class based on what they told me their parents did for work. Most of the interviewees at the public school had parents who worked in working-class or lower middle-class jobs. Their parents were secretaries, cashiers, nurses, a physical therapist's assistant, factory workers, hairdressers, house painters, day care workers, carpenters, a computer data entry specialist, and a few were unemployed. Interviewees from the private schools had parents who worked at middle- and upper-middle-class jobs. They included doctors, entrepeneurs, business managers, sales representatives, lawyers, artists, corporate executives, contractors, and psychologists. Two girls from the public high school also had parents in middle-class jobs. One father was a manager and one was a lawyer. Throughout the book I use "working-class" to refer to the first group of adolescents and "middle-class" to refer to the second. These categories of class, however, are not objective measures. The first group might more accurately be both working- and lower-middle-class and the second group be upper-middle-class. I make these class divisions to indicate that there were significant socioeconomic differences between these groups that affected their adolescent experience.

About three-quarters of the working-class students identified their religion as Catholic, although many said they did not practice. Eight of the middle-class interviewees were Jewish. Five interviewees said they were practicing

Protestants. One was Buddhist, and the rest said that they were not religious or had no religion.

Forty-five of the teenagers were white, four Asian-American and six Latino/Chicano. About twenty percent of my interviewees were nonwhite. I did not interview any African-American students because they were few in the school populations from which I was sampling and do not experience a drop in self-esteem the same way that girls in other groups do. Throughout the book, I do not generalize to all teens. I make comparisons based on class and gender, and I pay attention to racial, ethnic, and religious differences where they occur, although I do not have large enough samples to generalize about each group. Finally, although I asked my original questions about sexuality and love relationships in a way that did not assume sexual preference or the gender of one's partners, all the teens presented themselves to me as heterosexual. Thus, although I draw on the literature about lesbian and gay identity and gay and lesbian teens, this is a study of the pubertal and first sexual experiences of teens who are identified as heterosexual while in high school. Cook, Boxer, and Herdt suggest that not long ago this would have been a "complete" study of adolescents because "self-identification as gay or lesbian *during adolescence*, may be part of a unique developmental pattern found only in the current generations of some homosexual youth…"[196] They also remind us that many gay and lesbian teens and adults have some early heterosexual experience.

131

INTERVIEW QUESTIONS.

The interview itself consisted of about fifty open-ended questions. (See Interview Schedule below.) I did not ask every teen every interview question, but I asked most of the questions to all the teens. The interview varied depending on the teen's willingness to talk,[197] the extent of their experience with puberty and sex, and the direction they pushed the interview. Some interviews took the form of a conversation between the teen and me, and others took a question and answer format.

I asked every teen a series of question to assess their sense of self and their self-worth. These questions were (1) Tell me about your self/describe yourself. (2) Do you like yourself/are you happy with yourself? (3) Describe yourself at age ten? (4) Do you like yourself better now or at age ten? And why? (5) What kind of things make you feel good about yourself, proud of yourself? What makes you feel bad about yourself? I asked question one, as a general question to get the interviewee's general description of him or herself before I muddied the waters with any more specific questions. I asked question two because it is the question that the AAUW study uses to assess self-esteem.[198] Although I took interviewees qualitative answers and did not force them to respond on a Lickert scale, I found differences in what the AAUW calls self-esteem using this question. Girls were less likely to say that they were happy with themselves without qualification and more likely to say outright that they were not happy with themselves. (See Table One.)

Table One
Happy with Self?

	Without Qualification	With Qualification	Not Happy With Self	Total
Girls	11	17	4	32
Working Class	8	7	3	
Middle Class	3	10	1	
Boys	22	1	0	23
Working Class	11	0	0	
Middle Class	11	1	0	
Total	33	18	4	55

I asked questions three and four because Gilligan and colleagues assert that girls are happier with themselves and more free when they are pre-adolescent.[199] I also used it to judge whether or not interviewees perceived a drop in self-worth since they had become teens. Finally, question five was used to see what adolescents themselves thought raised or lowered their self-esteem. From these five questions I discerned the general level of self-esteem of each of the interviewees.

I followed these questions up with questions that assessed how agentic each interviewee felt, to see if they felt like someone who acted, accomplished, and engaged with the world. These questions reached a sense of self that most self-esteem literature does not take into account but that the less empirical psychoanalytic literature does. The questions I asked were "Can you describe an important goal that you set for yourself and how you achieved that goal? Did you ever have a goal that you were unable to achieve?" "Do you play any sports? Or dance or cheer or do gymnastics or swim or run or do aerobics or lift weights? Why do you do this activity? Do you enjoy it? What do you like about it?" "What are your hobbies?" "What abilities do you have that you are confident about?" "Are there things you would like to do but are afraid to? Why?" "What is one of the most difficult things you have ever had to do?" "What things come easy to you? What are you good at?" I also asked questions about school—whether or not one liked it, did well in school, or ever skipped school. These questions about school probed interviewees' lives for areas where they might be agentic.

Also in this early part of the interview I asked the interviewees to tell me what they daydreamed about. I asked this question as a way of trying to access some part of each interviewee's fantasy life. Because psychoanalytic theory finds fantasy so important in interpreting selves, I hoped that asking about daydreams would be a way to get at some fantasies of adolescents, even if they were conscious ones. This question worked well with some girls, who described elaborate daydreams of varying content, but less well with other girls and with boys, who often said "Daydream?" or "I don't daydream," as if it were a waste of time and/or unmasculine.

In the next part of interview I asked the adolescents to describe their parents and their relationships with their parents. Again, asking these questions was motivated by the insights of psychoanalytic theorists who assert the importance of parents and parent-child relationships in shaping children's selves.

Next, I asked a series of questions about bodies and puberty, starting with general questions like "How would you describe the way you look? Do you like the way that you look?" in order to examine body image. I asked not just if interviewees liked their appearance, but asked them to describe their appearance in order to see which parts of their bodies and appearances they would comment on, to see which had significance to them. I then moved into asking specific questions about puberty. I began by asking how they learned about puberty and sex, and from whom they learned it. I then asked a series of questions about some of the experiences that comprise puberty—breast development, menstruation, and shaving (hair growth) for girls, and voice change and shaving for boys.[200] I also asked boys about muscle development and the importance of developing muscles.[201]

I followed up the questions of "What happened when you started your period/started shaving/your voice changed/you developed breasts with the question, "How did you feel." Asking about feelings after these events was important for evaluating the effect of the pubertal event on the interviewee's sense of self. I also asked both boys and girls what else they thought concerned adolescents during this period. I asked a few interviewees, boys and girls, about masturbation when I began interviewing, but I found that it made them, particularly the girls, uncomfortable. I stopped asking about masturbation, although several interviewees brought it up on their own during the interview.

Next, I moved on to asking about sex education, as a transition into the topic of sex. Asking about sex education allowed me to gauge how much knowledge an individual interviewee had about sex, their general perspective on it, and how comfortable they would be discussing it more personally. I then began asking about intimate relationships, knowing that most teens are serially monogamous and have sex in these types of relationships.[202] If a discussion of a boyfriend or girlfriend did not lead to a discussion of sex, I then asked outright if the interviewee had had sex. If the answer was yes, I followed up by asking about the experience, and, importantly, the feelings they had following the experience. If the answer was no, I asked how they thought they might decide to have sex in the future, and then asked about their feelings about sex—what did they look forward to and what were they anxious about? Again, questions about how teens feel about their sexual experiences have rarely been asked in previous research on teenage sex.[203]

By way of ending the interview on an easier subject and as a way to estimate how agentic or subjective interviewees felt about their life as a whole, I asked a series of questions about their futures. I asked them to imagine their lives in five years and in twenty-five years, because being able to imagine one's possibilities, being able to dream, seems like an important necessary step in being agentic. I also asked more basic questions that related directly to agency—"What do you want to do when you are finished with high school?" "What do you want to accomplish in your life?" "What do you want your life to be like?" I knew that these answers would vary tremendously by class and suspected that they would also vary by gender.[204]

Finally, I asked interviewees why they participated, what they thought of the interview, if they thought I should have asked something that I did not, and if they had anything else to add. The answers to these questions helped me to see any problems in the interview and asked the interviewees to contribute to the research.[205] These questions also brought the interviews to a close.

ANALYZING AND EDITING.

In analyzing the data, I relied on a grounded theory approach.[206] In other words, I moved between theory and data in discerning the patterns in the interviews. After transcribing the interviews and reading through them several times, I coded (categorized and counted) each one for forty-five different themes. I also grouped interviews by general types—those who had sex, those who had not, those who gave positive and those who gave negative descriptions of self, and of course by class and gender—and read through them again in these groups looking for patterns. Some of these themes or patterns emerged inductively from data; that is, as I read through the interviews I found that many interviewees were saying something similar, and I then went back through all the interviews looking for those specific themes. Some of the themes I coded for based on the theoretical material presented in Chapter Two. Because the interview questions were theoretically driven, many of these themes were organized by the questions I had asked. The analysis presented throughout the book comes from this work and is organized according to these themes and patterns.

When I include excerpts from the interviews, the reader should consider them to be representative of the interviews in general. In presenting the interview material I have tried to select the most representative quotations from interviews, and when possible to give the reader examples of the exceptions or "outliers." I tried to avoid overuse or underuse any particular interview or set of interviews throughout the book. However, some interviewees may be represented more in one chapter and less in others. For example, adolescents who said they had never had sexual intercourse are quoted less frequently than those who did in the chapters on sex.

The interview material that I present is somewhat edited. By this I mean, that I have removed a few "umm's," "ah's," "you know's," "like's," and a few stutters that get in the way of understanding what the interviewee is saying. Adolescent speech tends to be dense with these phrases. However, I have not cleaned up the quotations completely because I wanted to convey the texture of teenage speech (which the reader may notice varies somewhat by class and gender). Also, "like's" and "you know's" sometimes indicate where adolescents are reluctant, unclear, debating what to say, or confused. The pauses, starts and stops, and stutters, all help to indicate how the adolescents feel about what they are saying.[207] In none of my editing did I change words or delete words that would change meanings. I have, however, changed all identifying information to protect the anonymity of my interviewees. Where names of interviewees occur, they are pseudonyms, and I have also in a very few cases given two pseudonyms to one interviewee to avoid the possibility of combining their excerpts and jeopardizing their anonymity. Occasionally, I have added a word in brackets to make the interviewees' meanings more clear.

135

INTERVIEW SCHEDULE

BOYS AND GIRLS:

age
grade
parents' marital status
parents' jobs
religion
brothers and sisters
race/ethnicity

Self and Agency.

Tell me about yourself. (How would you describe yourself?)
Are you happy with yourself? Why or why not? What do you like and dislike?

Describe yourself at age ten. Do you like yourself more or less or the same now? Why?

What kind of things make you feel good about yourself, proud of yourself? What makes you feel bad about yourself?

Can you describe an important goal that you set for yourself and how you achieved that goal? Did you ever have a goal that you were unable to achieve? Why?

Do you play any sports? Or dance or cheer or do gymnastics or swim or run or do aerobics or lift weights? Why do you do this activity? Do you enjoy it? Why or why not? What do you like about it?

What are your hobbies?

What kinds of things do you daydream about?

What abilities do you have that you are confident about?

Are there things you would like to do but are afraid to? What? Why?

What is one of the most difficult things you have ever had to do?

What things come easy to you? What are you good at?

Parents.

How would you describe/tell me about your mother? Your father?

What is your relationship like with each of them?

School and agency:

Do you like school? Why or why not?

How do you feel about how well you do in school?

Has this changed since you were a kid?

Do you ever skip school? Why or why not?

What are your favorite subjects?

Body image.

How would you describe the way you look?

Do you like the way that you look?

Do others think you are attractive?

What specifically do you like/dislike about your body?

What parts, what things it can do?

Do you diet? Why? How?

Puberty.

How did you learn about puberty and sex?

Parents: What did they tell you? How old were you? What did you think/feel then? How did you react?

What advice has your mother given you about boys? What did you think? What has your father said?

Friends: What did they say? What did you think/feel/do?
Siblings: What did they say? What did you think/feel/do?
Other: What did you think?

GIRLS ONLY:

Some girls are happy when they develop breasts, some are self-conscious about it, and some don't care or don't notice. What was it like for you?

Did it make any difference in your life, in what you did or didn't do?

Do you shave? When did you start shaving? Why? Did anyone help/teach you? What did they say or do? What did you think about it? What did it mean to you?

Have you started your period? (or Do you have periods?) When did you start your period? What happened? How did you feel about it then?

What do you think about having periods now?

Do you use tampons? When did you start using them? How did you learn how to do it? Was it easy or difficult?

Some girls worry about going swimming, wearing shorts, or playing sports when they have their period. Has having periods changed what you do or feel you can do?

Have you gone to the gynecologist? What was it like? Were you scared?

What kinds of things do you think younger girls worry about during puberty? Did you worry about these things?

Do you think girls are comfortable with their bodies? Boys?

What difference do you think growing up/becoming a teenager has made in your life?

139

BOYS ONLY:

Some boys "work out" a lot and think it is important to have muscles. What do you think? Why is it (un)important?

How old were you when your voice changed? What was it like? How did you feel about it? Did it make you act any differently?

Do you shave? When did you start shaving? Why? Did anyone help/teach you? What did they say or do? What did you think about it? What did it mean to you?

What kinds of things do you think young boys worry about in puberty? Did you worry about these things?

BOYS AND GIRLS:

Do you think boys are comfortable with their bodies? Girls?

What difference do you think growing up/becoming a teenager has made in your life?

Sex education.

Tell me about sex ed. in school?
What do you think of it? Is it useful? Why? Why not?
What would you tell a younger girl about sex?
How would you teach a sex education class if you were the teacher?
What do you think about the school distributing condoms?

Relationships.

(Have you kissed someone?) How old were you when you first kissed some-one? Who? What was it like? What did you think about it afterwards?
Are you in a relationship now? How did you get together? How long have you been together?
Describe your boyfriend/girlfriend. What do you like about him/her? What is your relationship like? How does he/she make you feel about yourself?
IF NO: Would you like to be in a relationship? Why or why not? What do you think you would like or dislike about being in a relationship?
Do you have sex with this person? Why did you begin having sex? What is it like? Do you like it? How do you feel before? Afterwards?

Sex.

What do your friends say about sex? About boys/girls?
What do *you* think?
Have you had sex?
How did you/would you decide to have sex the first time?
What happened? Was it what you expected? Do you remember what you did right afterwards? What did you do the next day? Did it change anything in your life afterwards? What was your relationship with the boy/girl like after-wards?
Did you use birth control? Who decided to or not to?
What would you do if you got pregnant?
Has sex gotten better, worse, or different since the first time? How has it changed? How have you changed?
OR
What do you think it will be like? What do you expect?
What do you look forward to? What do you feel uneasy or apprehensive about?
Do you think that sex is different for boys and girls? How?
Many girls have talked about how it is hard for girls to say no when a boy wants them to have sex and they don't really want to. Why do you think this is so hard for girls?

Future and agency.

What is an important decision you had to make? How did you make it? Who or what influenced you or helped you to make that decision?

What do you want to do when you're finished with high school? How are you going to achieve that? What are your plans?

What do you think your future will be like? How do you imagine your life in five years? In twenty-five years? What do you think you'll have to do to get this future?

Do you want to get married? When? Why or why not?

Do you want to be a mother/father?

What kind of work do you want to do?

Tell me about your life as a whole. What do you want your life to be like? What do you want to accomplish in your life?

End.

Why did you volunteer? What did you think of it? Anything to add?
Friends who would participate?

ENDNOTES

1. Simmons and Blyth (1987), AAUW (1991).

2. See Lillian Rubin's *Erotic Wars: Whatever Happened to the Sexual Revolution* (1990).

3. Oakley (1981), Personal Narratives Group (1989).

4. Brooks-Gunn (1990), Brooks-Gunn and Petersen (1984).

5. Other interviewers, men and women, have encountered this problem as well (Thompson [1984], Gaddis and Brooks-Gunn [1985]).

6. Thompson (1984, p. 351).

7. See Rubin (1983) for a similar finding about adult men and women.

8. Thorne (1993, p. 168).

9. Empirical evidence also suggests that adolescent boys are comfortable talking to women about sex. Researchers find innercity adolescent males, some who had been sexually abused and some who had not, prefer and are more comfortable with a female interviewer. Of those who had been abused, all preferred a female interviewer whether their abuse had been by a male or female. Of those who had not been abused, fifty-

three percent said they did not have a preference. Although this study was conducted with a clinical population, it lends some support to the argument that teenage boys are comfortable talking about sex with female interviewers.

10. Three interviewees, two girls and a boy, referred to the interview as a whole or parts of it as being like talking to the doctor.

11. Johnson (1963).

12. Personal Narratives Group (1989), Warren (1988).

13. Chan (1994, p. 89).

14. AAUW (1991), Brown and Gilligan (1992), Gilligan (1991), Gilligan, Rogers, and Tolman (1991), Gilligan, Lyons, and Hammer (1989), Hancock (1989), Orenstein (1994), Sadker and Sadker (1993).

15. See also the AAUW (1993) study of sexual harassment in schools. Adolescent girls are also found to be more depressed and to underestimate their competence in life skills (Petersen et al. [1991], Poole and Evans [1989]).

16. Specifically, compared to boys, white and Hispanic girls' self-esteem drops sharply between elementary school and high school. African-American girls' self-esteem does not drop (AAUW 1991). The AAUW study does not have data on Asian-American girls or Native American girls. However, Martinez and Dukes (1991) find lower self-esteem for Asian-American adolescent girls and Native American girls. Early research on race differences in self-esteem found that African-Americans did not have lower self-esteem than whites (Rosenberg and Simmons [1971], cited in Jensen et al. [1982]). Simmons et al. (1978) even found that black children had higher self-esteem than white children. This finding was counterintuitive. Researchers did not understand why racism had not affected African-Americans' self-esteem. Several answers were suggested to explain this. Jensen et al. (1982) suggest that class complicated these studies. Rosenberg and Simmons suggested that black children compare themselves to other black children not to white children, and thus their self-esteem does not suffer. Yet Simmons et al. (1978) suggest that even in desegregated schools black children have self-esteem equal to or higher than of white children. Finally, Martinez and Dukes (1991) conceptualize this as a problem of public domain versus private domain self-esteem. They find that nonwhite groups have lower public domain self-esteem, although as high or higher private domain self-esteem (Martinez and Dukes [1991]). See also Rosenberg (1979, 1989). For a look at self-esteem's connection to social problems that reverses the causality (low self-esteem causes social problems) see Mecca et al. (1989).

17. Brown and Gilligan (1992, p. 2).

18. Brown and Gilligan (1992, p. 2).

19. Brown and Gilligan (1992, p. 93).

20. See Mahoney (in press) for a critique of silence as passive and oppressed.

21. See Erikson (1950, 1968).

22. Gilligan (1982).

23. AAUW (1991).

24. Sadker and Sadker (1993).

25. How can these theorists neglect areas so central to adolescent life? Hartsock (1987) suggests that feminist academics neglect the body both empirically and theoretically. Feminists fear making claims about the body, because they are afraid that those claims will be turned against women as "essentialism." Instead, much feminist debate (the so-called feminist sex wars) has focused on sexual practices, asking which are

empowering and which are oppressive (Rubin [1984], MacKinnon [1987], Califia [1979], B. Ruby Rich [1986], Dworkin [1987, 1981]; Daly [1984], Campbell [1987], *MS* [1994]). Currently there is a trend in feminist theory of turning the body into a "text," preventing it from being essentialized but losing it as an experienced, lived body.

26. Laumann et al. (1994, p. 373).

27. See Simmons and Blyth (1987).

28. Aptheker (1989, p. 136).

29. Benjamin (1986, p. 87).

30. Freud (1923), Winnicott (1965), Stern (1985).

31. Schachtel (1959).

32. See also Apter (1990).

33. Blos (1962), Settlage (1976), Chodorow (1978).

34. Brooks-Gunn and Petersen (1984).

35. Apter (1990).

36. Laufer (1976).

37. Eme (1979).

38. Brownmiller (1984), Wolf (1991).

39. Lorde (1984, p. 53).

40. Laumann et al. (1994, p. 372).

41. Sholty et al. (1984).

42. See Benjamin (1988, 1986).

43. Focusing on the developmental phase of rapprochement, Benjamin suggests that the child is looking for *recognition* that she/he is a subject, an "I" who can "do." Recognition is a key element for the development of agency and desire in Benjamin's model. To recognize is "to affirm, validate, acknowledge, know, accept, understand, empathize, take in, tolerate, appreciate, see, identify with, find familiar,...love." (1988, p. 15). The father, whom both girls and boys see as exciting, outside, and free, and who is idealized as a representation of freedom, is crucial to this moment of development. Although both boys and girls wish to become desiring subjects, only boys, according to Benjamin, have complete access to the means of achieving this wish because only boys are able to identify with the father. Fathers respond to boys. The ability to identify with the father allows the boy to separate from mother and to avoid feelings of helplessness while also creating a representation of desire in which the boy finds himself as a subject or agent. The boy then psychically splits the father/men and the mother/women into the subject and object of desire. This attainment of subjectivity cannot be achieved for girls in the same way. In Benjamin's model, attainment of subjectivity is dependent on recognition by another who is a subject in her/his own right, and the mother is not such an other. The father also cannot recognize the girl as a subject who is "like him."

Thus, "when the girl realizes she cannot *be* the father, she wants to *have* the father" and to live vicariously through him. Here is the root of women's alienated desire, of women's desire being expressed as what Benjamin calls ideal love. The girl/woman cannot be the subjective, exciting, agentic owner of desire, and thus she achieves desire by basking in the glow of the idealized other. Ideal love often structures the loves and desires of a woman's life.

44. There are, however, several psychoanalysts who have examined adolescence, although many of them lose sight of the body and sexuality. (Blos [1962, 1970]; Deutsch [1944, 1945]; Erikson [1950, 1968]; Sullivan [1953], Laufer [1968, 1989], and Laufer and Laufer [1984]). This is particularly true of Erikson because of his focus on identity.

45. Gagnon and Simon (1973), Simon and Gagnon (1986).

46. Simon and Gagnon (1986, p. 98).

47. Simon and Gagnon (1986, p. 98).

48. Simon and Gagnon (1986, p. 99).

49. Connell (1995, p. 53).

50. Benjamin (1988, 1986).

51. Simmons and Blyth (1987), AAUW (1991).

52. For example, one middle-class girl described her father as "insecure about himself," and then proceeded to describe him using the language of psychology, "And he doesn't feel good about his job right now. He doesn't feel useful, and I don't know if that's true or if he's projecting." Working-class girls were more likely to say something like "He's a good guy, but sometimes he's moody."

53. Parker et al. (1995).

54. Belcastro (1985).

55. Chan (1994).

56. Savin-Williams and Rodriguez (1993). However, we also know that there are extremely high suicide rates among gay youth (Raymond [1994]).

57. Raymond (1994, p. 126).

58. Cook, Boxer and Herdt (1989). See also Thompson (1995).

59. Thorne (1993).

60. For a review of the literature on menarche see Grief and Ulman (1982) and Brooks-Gunn (1992).

61. Brooks-Gunn and Ruble (1982), Brooks-Gunn (1992).

62. Apter (1990) similarly finds "Whatever information a girl had been given, she felt ignorant about some aspect of menstruation. Either she felt she had not been given enough information about the underlying hormonal process, and complained about the length of time it had taken for her to associate mood swings with menstruation, or she felt it had come much sooner than she expected, and that she had not been told it could normally start, say, at twelve, or she felt she lacked practical information-how to avoid blood spots on clothes...or how to get a tampon 'all the way in,' that is, in the right position, and how you could tell it was right." (p. 38–9).

63. Lerner (1976).

64. See Ash (1980) for a further discussion of this issue.

65. Martin (1987) and Lee (1994).

66. See E. Martin (1987).

67. Ruble and Brooks-Gunn (1982), Brooks-Gunn (1992).

68. Simon and Gagnon (1986).

69. Brooks-Gunn and Petersen (1983), Brooks-Gunn (1992), Simmons and Blyth (1987).

70. Thorne (1994, p. 139).

71. Brooks-Gunn (1992)

72. Lakoff and Scherr (1984).

73. Cherrie Moraga (1983, p. 9).

74. Cherrie Moraga (1983, p. 4).

75. Thorne (1993, p. 146).

76. Lee (1994, p. 346).

77. Lee (1994).

78. Thorne (1993, p. 141).

79. Brooks-Gunn and Warren (1988, p. 1066).

80. However, Thorne and Luria's (1986) research and Best's (1983) suggests that children's social worlds contain some sexuality from as early as elementary school.

81. Apter (1990), Simmons and Blyth (1987).

82. Chernin (1985), Millman (1980).

83. Paxton et al. (1991), Duke-Duncan (1991), Rauste-von-Wright (1989), Silberstein (1987), Fisher (1986), Duncan et al. (1985).

84. Parker et al. (1995).

85. See also Toni Morrison's *The Bluest Eye* for an example of the pain involved in this standard.

86. They did not say this because I asked "Do you think you are fat?", but brought up the subject of their weight or size in a variety of places in the interview. When I asked them "Tell me about yourself," or about their goals, or to describe how they looked.

87. Silberstein et al. (1987, p. 94).

88. Silberstein et al. (1987, p. 91).

89. Silberstein et al. (1987).

90. See Attie, Brooks-Gunn and Petersen (1990) for a review of the literature on eating problems and disorders.

91. 2,500 teenage girls have breast reduction surgery a year. Another 21,500 teens, by far the majority of them girls, have other types of cosmetic surgery each year. (Rosen and Sheff-Cahan 1993).

92. Benjamin (1988).

93. Apter (1990).

94. Chan (1994).

95. Clearly the doing and the compliment are not necessarily "really" related, but to the teen girl they are.

96. There is some feminist research on women shaving. See Basow (1991).

97. Sometimes it is associated with a negative identification with mother as with Kelly who states that she did not cut herself until her mother knew she was shaving.

98. Erikson (1950, 1968), Offer (1969).

99. Gaddis and Brooks-Gunn (1985), Adegoke (1993), Downs and Fuller (1991).

100. Gaddis and Brooks-Gunn (1985).

101. Rosenbaum (1979).

102. Laumann et al. (1994, p. 81).

103. See Lyman (1987).

104. This defense may be unavailable to girls because adult female sexuality is also infantilizing.

105. Brooks-Gunn and Petersen (1983), Duke-Duncan (1981), Apter (1990), Brooks-Gunn (1992).

106. Petersen and Crockett (1985).

107. Thorne, (1993, p. 140).

108. For a discussion of the meaning and importance of these categories in teenage culture see Eckert (1989) and Gaines (1990).

109. Connell (1995), Hunter (1993), Hartley (1974).

110. Peter Blos (1962, p. 2).

111. Chilman (1983a) also makes this observation.

112. See Rosenbaum (1979) for an exception.

113. Brooks-Gunn (1992), Simmons and Blyth (1987), Brooks-Gunn (1984), Tobin-Richards, Boxer, and Petersen (1983), Simmons, Blyth, and McKinney (1983), Simmons et al. (1979).

114. Brooks-Gunn and Warren (1989), Brooks-Gunn and Warren (1988), Simmons and Blyth (1987).

115. Chilman (1983a) suggests that we need "somewhat open-ended, in-depth clinical studies that use both intensive interviews and appropriate tests that seek to understand more about the adolescent as a whole human being *who feels as well as thinks, values, and behaves*" (italics mine, p. 28). She goes on to say that with few exceptions "almost none of the research takes a developmental view of adolescent sexuality in the context of the feelings of teenagers about themselves, their families, and their society" (p. 30).

116. Brooks-Gunn and Furstenberg (1989), Furstenberg et al. (1987), Hayes (1987), Hofferth and Hayes (1987), Zelnick and Kantner (1980).

117. Padilla and Baird (1991), Wright et al. (1990).

118. Brooks-Gunn and Furstenberg (1989, p. 249).

119. These terms are probably specific to some subcultures of teenagers. The working-class teenagers used them more then the middle-class teenagers. Ruth Horowitz (1983) finds that urban Chicano youth in the midwest use these terms as well. Thorne's (1993) study (in Michigan and California) finds that children in early adolescence use the term "goin' with."

120. Thorne and Luria (1986).

121. Ward and Taylor (1994) also find white boys complain about their heterosexual relationships and give them very different meanings than girls do.

122. Benjamin (1988, 1986).

123. Raymond (1994), Cook, Boxer, Herdt (1989).

124. Martin (1988), McRobbie and McCabe (1981).

125. Hochschild (1994).

126. Thompson (1994, p. 245).

127. Rubin (1985).

128. Laumann et al. (1994, p. 371).

129. Laumann et al. (1994) found that "only about three percent of women said that physical pleasure was their main reason for having first intercourse, compared to four times as many men who said this (12 percent) (p. 329).

130. See Hayes (1987). However, I find these numbers for girls a bit low when comparing them to my sample in which of girls who were an average age of about sixteen, half had sex. Many said they had sex at fourteen, fifteen, and sixteen years old.

131. Brooks-Gunn and Furstenberg (1989, p. 256).

132. Thompson (1984, 1990) has investigated this question, but she has only interviewed girls, and so her claims about gender differences in this decision making are weak.

133. Sanday (1990, p. 113).

134. Laumann et al. (1994) found that about one-fourth of all women reported that they did not want to have sex the first time (p. 328).

135. Cook, Boxer, and Herdt (1989, p. 26).

136. Chilman (1983a).

137. Thompson (1990, p. 345).

138. Hite (1976), Thompson (1990).

139. Tolman (1994).

140. Thompson (1990, p. 351).

141. Boys establish a sexual identity earlier, an average age of fifteen (Anderson, 1990; Cook, Boxer, and Herdt 1989).

142. Fullilove et al. (1990).

143. Moffatt (1989, italics in original, p. 199).

144. Person (1980).

145. All quotes are from *Time* (April 5, 1993, p. 41).

146. See brief review by Treboux and Busch-Rossnagel (1991).

147. T. Fisher (1989).

148. There is much research on teen contraceptive use. Some general findings are: the older an adolescent is the more likely she/he is to use contraception and to use it correctly (Zelnick, Kantner, and Ford [1981]). Low income, low educational aspirations, troubled relationships with parents, no sex education (although this is debated) are all thought to lead teens to have sex at an earlier age and to make them less likely to use contraception (Brooks-Gunn and Furstenberg [1989], Brooks-Gunn [1992]). Girls know more about specific contraceptives than boys do, and girls' contraceptive knowledge has been studied more frequently (Brooks-Gunn and Furstenberg [1989]).

149. Ward and Taylor (1994, p. 63).

150. Fullilove et al. (1990, p. 52–3).

151. See Horowitz (1983).

152. Gavey (1993).

153. Simon and Gagnon (1986).

154. See Hochschild (1983) for a theory of emotion management.

155. Brown and Gilligan (1992).

156. See p. 120–121 for example, in Brown and Gilligan.

157. Thompson (1994, p. 228).

158. From preliminary interviews.

159. Freud (1905), Chodorow (1978), Benjamin (1988), Stoller (1985), Lerner, (1976).

160. Benjamin (1988).

161. Many psychoanalysts find that adolescent parental relations are a replaying of early childhood issues. (See Chodorow 1978, especially Chapter 8, Blos 1962, Deustch 1944).

162. Benjamin (1988), Chodorow (1978).

163. I edited this story for the sake of space and for the confidentiality of this boy and his family.

164. Benjamin (1988, p. 105).

165. Chodorow and Contratto (1982).

166. Chodorow (1978).

167. Chodorow (1978).

168. Blauner (1993).

169. Contratto (1987).

170. Benjamin (1988), Contratto (1987).

171. Apter (1990).

172. Rubin (1976).

173. Apter (1990), Chodorow (1978).

174. Chodorow (1978, p. 136).

175. See Chapter Six for expanded discussion of this issue.

176. Collins (1990).

177. Fine (1992).

178. Madeleine Blais' (1995).

179. I do not suggest that all romantic love or all desires to marry are the same as ideal love or are "bad" for girls' agency. However, the way teenage girls talk about marriage closely resemble ideal love and often come with a story of being saved.

180. Gilligan (1990), Hancock (1989).

181. Brooks-Gunn and Ruble (1983).

182. Apter (1990).

183. Chodorow (1978).

184. Shopper, (1979).

185. It is unclear from my data if mothers can help daughters to desire, that is to want sex, to know how to ask for sexual pleasure. I did not hear any accounts of this even from Erin or Samantha.

186. Fine (1988), Harper (1983), Thompson (1990).

187. Fine (1988).

188. Thompson (1990) and Fine (1988).

189. Thompson (1990, p. 359).

190. Ward and Taylor (1994).

191. Thorne (1993, p. 172).

192. Irvine (1994, p. 21).

193. Harper (1983, p. 232).

194. Laumann et al. (1994), Gavey (1993), Hite (1976), Fischer (1989), Sholty et al. (1984).

195. Brown and Gilligan (1992), Orenstein (1994), Tolman (1994), Thompson (1984, 1990, 1994).

196. Cook, Boxer, and Herdt (1989, p. 3).

197. I did not push reluctant subjects very hard out of respect for them and because of the subject matter.

198. AAUW (1991).

199. Brown and Gilligan (1992), Hancock (1989).

200. Brooks-Gunn (1992).

201. Glassner (1987).

202. Thompson (1984).

203. Chilman (1983a, 1983b).

204. Rubin (1976), MacLeod (1987), Marini and Brinton (1984).

205. Oakley (1981).

206. Glaser and Straus, (1967).

207. Blauner (1987).

151

REFERENCES

AAUW. (1991). *Shortchanging girls, shortchanging America.* Available from AAUW.

Adegoke, Alfred. (1993). The experience of spermarche among selected adolescent boys in Nigeria. *Journal of Youth and Adolescence.* 22: 201–209.

Anderson, Dennis. (1990). Homosexuality in adolescence. *Atypical Adolescence and Sexuality*, Max Sugar, ed. New York: W. W. Norton.

Apter, Terri. (1990). *Altered Loves.* New York: St. Martin's Press.

Aptheker, Bettina. (1989). *Tapestries of Life: Women's Work, Women's Consciousness and the Meaning of Daily Experience.* Amherst, MA: University of Massachusetts Press.

Ash, Mildred. (1980). The misnamed female sex organ. In *Women's Sexual Development*, edited by Martha Kirkpatrick. New York: Plenum Press.

Attie, Ilana, and Jeanne Brooks-Gunn, and Anne C. Petersen. (1990). A developmental perspective on eating disorders and eating problems. In *The Handbook of Developmental Psychopathology*, edited by Lewis and Miller. New York: Plenum Press.

REFERENCES

Basow, Susan. (1991). The hairless ideal: women and their body hair. *Psychology of Women Quarterly*. 15: 83–96.

Benjamin, Jessica. (1991). Father and daughter: identification with difference—a contribution to gender heterodoxy. *Psychoanalytic Dialogues*, 1:3, 277–299.

Benjamin, Jessica. (1988). *The Bonds of Love*. New York: Pantheon Books.

Benjamin, Jessica. (1986). A desire of one's own: psychoanalytic feminism and intersubjective space. In *Feminist Studies/Critical Studies*, edited by Teresa de Lauretis. Bloomington, IN: Indiana University Press.

Berkovitz, Irving. (1979). Effects of secondary school experience on adolescent female development. In *Female Adolescent Development*, edited by Max Sugar. New York: Brunner Mazel.

Best, Raphaela. (1983). *We've All Got Scars: What Boys and Girls Learn in Elementary School*. Bloomington, IN: Indiana University Press.

Blais, Madeleine. (1995). *In These Girls, Hope is a Muscle*. New York: Atlantic Monthly Press.

Blauner, Bob. (1993). Mama's boy: a memoir. Unpublished manuscript

Blauner, Bob. (1987). Editing first person sociology. *Qualitative Sociology*. 10: 46–64.

Blos, Peter. (1962). *On Adolescence: A Psychoanalytic Interpretation*. New York: The Free Press.

Blos, Peter. (1970). *The Young Adolescent*. New York: The Free Press.

Blume, Judy. (1971). *Then Again, Maybe I Won't*. New York: Dell Publishing Co.

Brooks-Gunn, Jeanne. (1984). The psychological significance of different pubertal events to young girls. *Journal of Early Adolescence*. 4:4, 315–327.

Brooks-Gunn, Jeanne. (1987). Pubertal processes and girls' psychological adaptation. In *Biological-Psychosocial Interactions in Early Adolescence*, edited by Richard Lerner and Terry Foch. Hillsdale, NJ: Lawrence Erlbaum Associates.

Brooks-Gunn, Jeanne. (1990). Overcoming barriers to adolescent research on pubertal and reproductive development. *Journal of Youth and Adolescence*. 19: 425–440.

Brooks-Gunn, Jeanne. (1992). The impact of puberty and sexual activity upon the health and education of adolescent girls and boys. In *Sex Equity and Sexuality in Education*, edited by Susan Shurberg Klein. Albany: State University of New York Press.

Brooks-Gunn, Jeanne and Frank F. Furstenberg. (1989). Adolescent sexual behavior. Special issue: children and their development: knowledge base, research agenda, and social policy application. *American Psychologist* 44: 249–257.

Brooks-Gunn, Jeanne and Anne Petersen. (1983). *Girls at Puberty: Biological and Psychosocial Perspectives*. New York: Plenum Press.

Brooks-Gunn, Jeanne and Anne Petersen. (1984). Problems in studying and defining pubertal events. *Journal of Youth and Adolescence*. 13: 181–196.

Brooks-Gunn, Jeanne, and Diane Ruble. (1982). The development of menstrual-related beliefs and behaviors during adolescence. *Child Development*. 53: 1567–1577.

Brooks-Gunn, Jeanne, and Diane Ruble. (1983). The experience of menarche from a developmental perspective. In *Girls at Puberty: Biological and Psychosocial Perspectives*, edited by J. Brooks-Gunn and A. Petersen. New York: Plenum.

Brooks-Gunn, Jeanne and Michelle Warren. (1988). The psychological significance of secondary sexual characteristics in nine to eleven-year-old girls. *Child Development.* 59: 1061–1069.

Brooks-Gunn, Jeanne and Michelle Warren. (1989). Biological and social contributions to negative affect in young adolescent girls. *Child Development.* 60: 40–55.

Brown, Lyn Mikel and Carol Gilligan. (1992). *Meeting at the Crossroads: Women's Psychology and Girls' Development.* Cambridge: Harvard University Press.

Brownmiller, Susan. (1984). *Femininity.* New York: Simon and Shuster.

Califia, Pat. (1979). Unraveling the sexual fringe: a secret side of lesbian sexuality. *The Advocate.* December 27.

Campbell, Beatrix. (1987). A feminist sexual politics: now you see it, now you don't. In *Sexuality: A Reader,* edited by Feminist Review. London: Virago Press.

Carroll, Jannell, Kari Volk, and Janet Hyde. (1985). Differences between males' and females' motives for engaging in sexual intercourse. *Archives of Sexual Behavior.* 14:2, 131–139.

Chan, Connie. (1994). Asian-American adolescents: issues in the expression of sexuality. In *Sexual Cultures and the Construction of Adolescent Identities,* edited by Janice Irvine. Philadelphia: Temple University Press.

Chernin, Kim. (1985). *The Hungry Self: Women, Eating, and Identity.* New York: Perennial Library.

Chilman, Catherine S. (1983a). *Adolescent Sexuality in a Changing American Society.* Bethesda MD: U. S. Department of Health, Education, and Welfare.

Chilman, Catherine S. (1983b). The development of adolescent sexuality. *Journal of Research and Development in Education.* 16:2, 16–26.

Chodorow, Nancy and Susan Contratto. (1982). The fantasy of the perfect mother. In *Rethinking the Family* edited by Barrie Thorne with Marilyn Yalom. New York: Longman.

Chodorow, Nancy. (1978). *The Reproduction of Mothering.* Berkeley, CA: University of California Press.

Chodorow, Nancy. (1992). Heterosexuality as a compromise formation: Reflections on the psychoanalytic theory of sexual development. *Psychoanalysis and Contemporary Thought.* 15: 267–304

Clausen, John. (1975). The social meaning of differential physical and sexual maturation. In *Adolescence in the Life Cycle,* edited by Sigmund Dragster and Glen Elder. New York: Halsted Press.

Clausen, John. (1991). Adolescent competence and the shaping of the life course. *American Journal of Sociology.* 96: 805–42.

Coles, Robert and Geoffrey Stokes. (1985). *Sex and the American Teenager.* New York: Harper and Row.

Connell, R. W. (1995). *Masculinities.* Berkeley, CA: University of California Press.

Contratto, Susan. (1987). Father presence in female psychological development. In *Advances in Psychoanalytic Sociology.* edited by Jermone Rabow, Gerald Platt, and Marion Goldman. Malabar, FL: Krieger.

Cook, Judith, Andrew Boxer, and Gilbert Herdt. (1989). First homosexual Experiences reported by gay and lesbian youth in an urban community. Presented at the Annual Meetings of the American Sociology Association.

REFERENCES

Daly, Mary. (1984). *Pure Lust: Elemental Feminist Philosophy*. Boston: Beacon Press.

de Beauvoir, Simone. (1952). The formative years. *The Second Sex*. New York: Random House.

Deustch, Helene. (1944 and 1945). *The Psychology of Women, Volumes One and Two*. New York: Grune and Stratton.

Dinnerstein, Dorothy. (1976). *The Mermaid and the Minotaur: Sexual Arrangements and Human Malaise*. NY: Harper & Row.

Downs, Chris and M. J. Fuller. (1991). Recollections of spermarche: an exploratory investigation. *Current Psychology: Research and Reviews*. 10: 93–102.

Dreyer, Philip. (1982). Sexuality during adolescence. In *Handbook of Developmental Psychology*, edited by B. B. Wolman. NJ: Prentice Hall, 559–601.

Duke-Duncan, P., P. Ritter, S. Dornbusch, R. Gross, J. Carlsmith. (1985). The effects of pubertal timing on body image, school behavior, and deviance. *Journal of Youth and Adolescence*, 14: 227–235.

Duke-Duncan, Paula. (1991). Body image. In *Encyclopedia of Adolescence Vol. 1 and 2*, edited by R. Lerner, A. Petersen, J. Brooks-Gunn. New York: Garland Publishing.

Dworkin, Andrea. (1987). *Intercourse*. New York: The Free Press.

Eckert, Penelope. (1989). *Jocks and Burnouts: Social Categories and Identity in the High School*. New York: Teachers College, Columbia University.

Eme, R. F. (1979). Sex differences in childhood psychopathology: a review. *Psychological Bulletin*. 86: 574–595.

Erikson, Erik. (1950). *Childhood and Society*. New York: W. W. Norton.

Erikson, Erik. (1968). *Identity, Youth, and Crisis*. New York: Norton.

Fine, Michelle. (1992) *Disruptive Voices: The Possibilities of Feminist Research*. Ann Arbor: University of Michigan Press.

Fine, Michelle. (1988). Sexuality, schooling, and adolescent females: the missing discourse of desire. *Harvard Educational Review*. 58: 29–53.

Fine, Gary. (1987). The dirty play of little boys. In *Changing Men*, edited by Michael Kimmel. Newbury Park, CA: Sage Publications.

Fisher, Terri. (1989). An extension of the findings of moore, petersen, and furstenberg (1986) regarding family sexual communication and adolescent sexual behavior. *Journal of Marriage and the Family*. 51: 637–639.

Fisher, Seymour. (1989). *Sexual Images of the Self: The Psychology of Erotic Sensations*. New Jersey: Lawrence Earlbaum.

Fisher, Seymour. (1986). *Development and Structure of Body Image Vol. 1*.

Freud, Sigmund. (1905). *Three Theories of Sexuality*. New York: Basic Books, 1962.

Freud, Sigmund. (1923). *The Ego and the Id*. New York: Norton, 1960.

Freud, Sigmund. Female sexuality (1931). In *The Standard Edition of the Complete Psychological Works of Sigmund Freud v. XXI*, edited by James Strachey. London: Hogarth Press, 1961.

Fullilove, Mindy Thompson, Robert E. Fullilove, Katherine Haynes, and Shirley Gross. (1990). Black women and aids prevention: a view toward understanding gender rules. *The Journal of Sex Research*, 27:1, 47–64.

Furstenberg, Frank F., S. Morgan, K. Moore, and J. Peterson. (1987). Race differences in the timing of adolescent intercourse. *American Sociological Review*, 52: 511–518.

Gaddis, Alan and Jeanne Brooks-Gunn. (1985). The male experience of pubertal change. *Journal of Youth and Adolescence*, 14:1, 61–69.

Gagnon, John and William Simon. (1973). *Sexual Conduct*. Chicago: Aldine.

Gaines, Donna. (1990). *Teenage Wasteland: Suburbia's Dead End Kids*. NY: Harper Perennial.

Gargiulo, Janine, J. Brooks-Gunn, Ilana Attie, and Michelle Warren. (1987). Girls' dating behavior as a function of social context and maturation. *Developmental Psychology*, 23:5, 730–737.

Gavey, Nicola. (1993). Technologies and effects of heterosexual coercion. In *Heterosexuality: A feminism and psychology reader* edited by Sue Wilkinson and Celia Kitzinger. London: Sage Publications.

Gilligan, Carol. (1982). *In a Different Voice*. Cambridge, MA: Harvard University Press.

Gilligan, Carol. (1991). Joining the resistance: psychology, politics, girls and women. In *The Female Body: Figures, Styles, Speculations*, edited by L. Goldstein. Ann Arbor: University of Michigan.

Gilligan, Carol, Annie Rogers, and Deborah Tolman. (1991). *Women, Girls, and Psychotherapy: Reframing Resistance*. Cambridge: Harvard University Press.

Gilligan, Carol, Nona Lyons, and Trudy Hammer. (1989). *Making Connections*. Cambridge, MA: Harvard University Press.

Glaser, Barney and Anselm Straus. (1967) *The Discovery of Grounded Theory: Strategies for Qualitative Research*. Chicago: Aldine.

Glassner, Barry. (1987). Men and muscles. In *Changing Men*, edited by Michael Kimmel. Newbury Park, CA: Sage Publications.

Gold, Alice, Lorelei Brush, and Eve Sprotzer. (1980). Developmental changes in self-perceptions of intelligence and self-confidence. *Psychology of Women Quarterly*. 5: 231–241.

Greif, Esther Blank and Kathleen Ulman. (1982). The psychological impact of menarche on early adolescent females: a review of the literature. *Child Development*, 53: 1413–1430.

Hancock, Emily. (1989). *The Girl Within*. New York: Fawcett Publishers.

Harper, Ann. (1983). Teenage sexuality and public policy: an agenda for gender education. In *Families, Politics, and Public Policy: A Feminist Dialogue on Women and the State*, edited by Irene Diamond. New York: Longman.

Hartley, R. (1974). Sex-role pressures and the socialization of the male child. In *Men and Masculinity*, edited by J. H. Pleck and J. Sawyer. Englewood Cliffs, NJ: Prentice Hall, 7–13.

Hartsock, Nancy. (1987). The feminist standpoint: developing the ground for a specifically feminist historical materialism. In *Feminism and Methodology*, edited by Sandra Harding. Bloomington, IN: Indiana University Press.

C. D. Hayes. (1987). *Risking the Future: Adolescent Sexuality, Pregnancy, and Childbearing, Volume II*. Washington DC: National Academy of Science Press.

Hill and Lynch. (1983). In *Girls at Puberty: Biological and Psychosocial Perspectives*, edited by Jeanne Brooks-Gunn and Anne Petersen. New York: Plenum Press.

Hite, Shere. (1976). *The Hite Report: A Nationwide Study of Female Sexuality*. New York: Macmillan.

REFERENCES

Hochschild, Arlie. (1983). *The Managed Heart*. Berkeley, CA: University of California Press.

Hochschild, Arlie. (1994). The commercial spirit of intimate life and the abduction of feminism: signs form women's advice books. *Theory, Culture, and Society*. 11:2, 1–24

Hoffereth, S. L. and C. D. Hayes. (1987). *Risking the Future: Adolescent Sexuality, Pregnancy, and Childbearing, Volume II*. Washington DC: National Academy of Science Press.

Horowitz, Ruth. (1983). *Honor and the American Dream*. New Brunswick, NJ: Rutgers University Press.

Hunter, Allan. (1993). Same door, different closet: a heterosexual sissy's coming out party. In *Heterosexuality: A Feminism and Psychology Reader*, edited by Sue Wilkinson and Celia Kitzinger. London: Sage Publications.

Huston, Althea and Mildred Avery. (1990). The socialization context of gender role development in early adolescence. In *From Childhood to Adolescence*, edited by R. Montemayer, G. Adams, T. Gullotta. Newbury Park, CA: Sage Publications.

Irvine, Janice. (1994). *Sexual Cultures and the Construction of Adolescent Identities*. Philadelphia: Temple University Press.

Jensen, Gary, and C. S. White, and James Galliher. (1982). Ethnic status and adolescent self-evaluations: an extension of research on minority self-esteem. *Social Problems*, 30: 226–239.

Johnson, Miriam. (1963). Sex role learning in the nuclear family. *Child Development*. 34: 319–333.

Kaplan, Meg, Judith Becker, and Craig Tenke. (1991). Influence of abuse history on male adolescent self-reported comfort with interviewer gender. *Journal of Interpersonal Violence*. 6: 3–11.

Kestenberg, Judith. (1968). Outside and inside, male and female. *Journal of the American Psychoanalytic Association*, 16: 457–519.

Klein, Susan S. (1992). *Sex Equity and Sexuality in Education*. Albany: State University of New York Press.

Lakoff, Robin and Raquel Scherr. (1984). *Face Value: Politics of Beauty*. London: Routledge and Kegan Paul.

Laufer, Moses. (1976). The central masturbation fantasy, the final sexual organization, and adolescence. *Psychoanalytic Study of the Child*. 31: 297–316.

Laufer, Moses. (1989). Adolescent sexuality: a body/mind continuum. *Psychoanalytic Study of the Child*. 44: 281–294.

Laufer, Moses. (1968). The body image, the function of masturbation, and adolescence: problems of the ownership of the body. *Psychoanalytic Study of the Child*, 23: 114–137.

Laufer, Moses and M. Egle Laufer. (1984). *Adolescence and Developmental Breakdown: A Psychoanalytic View*. New Haven, CT: Yale University Press.

Laumann, Edward O., John H. Gagnon, Robert T. Michael, and Stuart Michaels. (1994). *The Social Organization of Sexuality: Sexual Practices in the United States*. Chicago: University of Chicago Press.

Lee, Janet. (1994). Menarche and the (hetero) sexualization of the female body. *Gender and Society*, 8:3, 343–362.

Lerner, H. E. (1976). Parental mislabeling of female genitals as a determinant of penis envy and learning inhibitions in women. *Journal of the American Psychoanalytic Association*, 24: 269–284.

Lorde, Audre. (1984). Uses of the erotic: the erotic as power. *Sister Outsider*. Freedom, CA: The Crossing Press.

Lyman, Peter. (1987). The fraternal bond as a joking relationship: a case study of the role of sexist jokes in male group bonding. In *Changing Men*, edited by Michael Kimmel. Newbury Park, CA: Sage Publications.

MacKinnon, Catharine. (1987). *Feminism Unmodified*. Cambridge, MA: Harvard University Press.

MacLeod, Jay. (1987). *Ain't No Makin' It: Leveled Aspirations in a Low-Income Neighborhood*. Boulder, CO: Westview Press.

Mahler, Margaret, Fred Pine, and Anni Bergmann. (1975). *The Psychological Birth of the Human Infant*. New York: Basic Books.

Marini, Margaret Mooney and Mary C. Brinton. (1984). Sex typing in occupational socialization. In *Sex Segregation in the Workplace: Trends, Explanations, Remedies*, edited by Barbara Reskin. Washington, DC: National Academy Press.

Martin, Emily. (1987). In *The Woman in the Body*. Boston: Beacon Press.

Martin, Karin. (1988). Of romance and rock stars: teenage girls and the question of desire. Division Three Thesis, Hampshire College.

Martinez, Rueben and Richard Dukes. (1991). Ethnic and gender differences in self-esteem. *Youth and Society*. 22: 318–338.

Mecca, Andrew, and Neil Smelser, and John Vasconcellos. (1989). *The Social Importance of Self-Esteem*. Berkeley, CA: University of California Press.

Millman, Marcia. (1980). *Such a Pretty Face*. New York: Norton.

Moffatt, Michael. (1989). *Coming of Age in New Jersey: College and American Culture*. New Brunswick: Rutgers University Press.

Moraga, Cherrie. (1983). *Loving in the War Years*. NY: Kitchen Table Women of Color Press.

Morrison, Toni. (1970). *The Bluest Eye*. New York: Washington Square Press.

MS. (1994). Where do we stand on pornography? *MS*. 4: 32–41.

Oakley, Ann. (1981). Interviewing women: a contradiction in terms. In *Doing Feminist Research*, edited by Helen Roberts. London: Routledge & Kegan Paul.

Offer, D. and J. Offer. (1969). *The Psychological World of the Teenager*. New York: Basic Books.

Orenstein, Peggy. (1994). *Schoolgirls: Young Women, Self-esteem and the Confidence Gap*. New York: Doubleday.

Padilla, Amado and Traci Baird. (1991). Mexican-American adolescent sexuality and sexual knowledge: an exploratory study. *Hispanic Journal of Behavioral Sciences*. 13: 95–104.

Parker, S., M. Nichter, M. Nichter, N. Vuckovic, C. Sims, C. Ritenbaugh. (1995). Body-image and weight concerns among African-American and white adolescent females—differences that make a difference. *Human Organization*. 54:103–114.

Patton, M. A. (1981). Self-concept and self-esteem: Factors in adolescent pregnancy. *Adolescence* 16: 765–778.

Paxton, Susan, Eleanor H. Wertheim, Kay Gibbons, George Szmukler, Lynne Hillier, and Janice L. Petrovich. (1991). Body image satisfaction, dieting beliefs, and weight loss behavior in adolescent girls and boys. *Journal of Youth and Adolescence.* 20:3, 361–379.

Person, Ethel. (1980). Sexuality as the mainstay of identity. *Signs* 5: 605–630.

Personal Narratives Group. (1989). *Interpreting Women's Lives.* Bloomington, IN: Indiana University Press.

Petersen, Anne. (1987). The nature of biological-psychosocial interactions: the sample case of early adolescence. In *Biological-Psychosocial Interactions in Early Adolescence,* edited by Richard Lerner and Terry Foch. Hillsdale, NJ: Lawrence Erlbaum Associates.

Petersen, Anne. (1988). Adolescent development. *American Review of Psychology,* 39: 583–607.

Petersen, Anne and L. J. Crockett. (1985). Pubertal timing and grade effects on adjust-ment. *Journal of Youth and Adolescence.* 14:191–206.

Petersen, Anne C., Pamela A. Sarigiani, and Robert E. Kennedy. (1991). Adolescent depression: why more girls? *Journal of Youth and Adolescence.* 20:2, 247–271.

Poole, Millicent and Glen T. Evans. (1989). Adolescents' self-perceptions of competence in life skill areas. *Journal of Youth and Adolescence.* 18:2, 147–173.

Quintanilla, Michael. (1991). Teenage girls becoming more sexually aggressive. *San Francisco Chronicle,* 28, June.

Rauste-von-Wright, Maijaliisa. (1989). Body image satisfaction in adolescent girls and boys: a longitudinal study. *Journal of Youth and Adolescence.* 18:1, 71–83.

Raymond, Diane. (1994). Homophobia, identity, and the meanings of desire: reflections on the cultural construction of gay and lesbian adolescent sexuality. In *Sexual Cultures and the Construction of Adolescent Identities,* edited by Janice Irvine. Philadelphia: Temple University Press.

Rich, B. Ruby. (1986). Feminism and sexuality in the 1980s. *Feminist Studies.* 12: 525–561.

Rich, Adrienne. (1980). Compulsory heterosexuality and lesbian existence. *Signs.* 5:4.

Ritvo, Samuel. (1984). Image and use of the body in psychic conflict: with special ref-erence to eating disorders in adolescence. *Psychoanalytic Study of the Child.* 39: 449–469.

Rosenbaum, Maj-Britt. (1979). Changing Body Image of the Adolescent Girl. In *Female Adolescent Development* edited by Max Sugar. NY: Brunner/Mazel Publishers.

Rosenberg, Morris. (1979). *Conceiving the Self.* New York: Basic Books, Inc.

Rosenberg, Morris. (1989). *Society and the Adolescent Self-Image.* Middletown, CT: Wesleyan University Press.

Rosenberg, Morris, Carmi Schooler, and Carrie Schoenbach. (1989). Self-esteem and adolescent problems: modeling reciprocal effects. *American Sociological Review,* 54: 1004–1018.

Rosenberg, Morris and Roberta Simmons. (1971). Black and white self-esteem: the urban school child. Washington, DC: American Sociological Association, Arnold and Caroline Rose Monograph Series.

Rubin, Lillian. (1985). *Just Friends.* New York: Harper and Row.

Rubin, Lillian. (1976). *Worlds of Pain.* New York: Basic Books.

160

Rubin, Lillian. (1983). *Intimate Strangers*. New York: Harper Books.

Rubin, Gayle. (1974). The traffic in women: notes on the political economy of sex. In *Women, Culture and Society* edited by Michelle Rosaldo and Louise Lamphere. Stanford, CA: Stanford University Press.

Rubin, Gayle. (1984). Thinking sex: notes for a radical theory of the politics of sexuality. In *Pleasure and Danger*, edited by Carol Vance. Boston: Routledge, Kegan Paul.

Ruble, D. N. and Jeanne Brooks-Gunn. (1982). The experience of menarche. *Child Development*. 53: 1557–1566.

Sadker, Myra and David Sadker. (1993). *Failing at Fairness: How America's Schools Cheat Girls*. New York: Charles Scribner and Sons.

Sanday, Peggy Reeves. (1990). *Fraternity Gang Rape*. New York: New York University Press.

Savin-Williams, Ritch C., and Richard G. Rodriguez. (1993). A developmental, clinical perspective on lesbian, gay, and bisexual youths. In *Adolescent Sexuality*, edited by Thomas P. Gullotta, Gerald R. Adams, and Raymond Montemayor. Newbury Park, CA: Sage Publications.

Schachtel, Ernest. (1959). On memory and childhood amnesia. In *Metamorphosis*. NY: Basic Books.

Settlage, Calvin. (1976). Panel reports: Psychology of women: late adolescence and early adulthood. *Journal of the American Psychoanalytic Association*. 24: 631–645.

Sholty, Mary Jo, Paul H. Ephross, S. Michael Plaut, Susan H. Fischman, Jane F. Charnas, and Carol A. Cody. (1984). Female orgasmic experience: a subjective study. *Archives of Sexual Behavior*. 13:2, 155–164.

Shopper, Moisy. (1979). "The (Re)Discovery of the Vagina and the Importance of the Menstrual Tampon." In *Female Adolescent Development*, edited by Max Sugar. NY: Brunner/Mazel Publishers, 214–233.

Silberstein, Lisa, and Ruth Striegel-Moore and Judith Rodin. (1987). Feeling fat: a woman's shame. In *The Role of Shame in Symptom Formation*, edited by Helen Block Lewis. Hillsdale, NJ: Earlbaum Associates.

Simmons, Roberta, and Leslie Brown, Diane Bush, and Dale Byth. (1978). Self-esteem and achievement of black and white adolescents. *Social Problems*, 26: 86–96.

Simmons, Roberta, Florence Rosenberg, and Morris Rosenberg. (1973). Disturbance in the self-image at adolescence. *American Sociological Review*. 39: 553–568

Simmons, Roberta, G., Dale A. Blyth, Edward F. Cleave, Diane Mitsch Bush. (1979). Entry into early adolescence: the impact of school structure, puberty, and early dating on self-esteem. *American Sociological Review*. 44: 948–967.

Simmons, R., D. Blyth, K. L. McKinney. (1983). The social and psychological effects of puberty on white females. In *Girls at Puberty: Biological and Psychosocial Perspectives*, edited by J. Brooks-Gunn and A. Petersen. New York: Plenum.

Simmons, R. and D. Blyth. (1987). *Moving into Adolescence: The Impact of Pubertal Change and School Context*. New York: Aldine de Gruyter.

Simon, William and John Gagnon. (1986). Sexual scripts: permanence and change. *Archives of Sexual Behavior*, 15:2, 97–120.

Smolowe, Jill. (1993). Sex with a scorecard. *Time*, 5, April.

Stern, Daniel. (1985). *The Interpersonal World of the Child: A View from Psychoanalysis and Developmental Psychology*. New York: Basic Books.

Stoller, Robert. (1985). *Presentations of Gender*. New Haven, CT: Yale University Press.

Sullivan, Harry Stack. (1953). *The Interpersonal Theory of Psychiatry*. New York: Norton.

Thompson, Sharon. (1984). Search for tomorrow: feminism and the reconstruction of teen romance. In *Pleasure and Danger* edited by Carol Vance. Boston: Routledge Kegan Paul.

Thompson, Sharon. (1990). Putting a big thing into a little hole: teenage girls' accounts of sexual initiation. *Journal of Sex Research* 27:3, 341–361.

Thompson, Sharon. (1994). What friends are for: on girls' misogyny and romantic fusion. In *Sexual Cultures and the Construction of Adolescent Identities*, edited by Janice Irvine. Philadelphia: Temple University Press.

Thompson, Sharon. (1995). *Going All the Way*. NY: Hill & Wang.

Thorne, Barrie. (1993). *Gender Play*. New Brunswick, NJ: Rutgers University Press.

Thorne, Barrie and Zella Luria. (1986). Sexuality and gender in children's daily worlds. *Social Problems*, 33: 176–190.

Tobin-Richards, M., A. Boxer, and A. Petersen. (1983). Earl adolescents' perceptions of their physical development. In *Girls at Puberty: Biological and Psychosocial Perspectives*, edited by J. Brooks-Gunn and A. Petersen. New York: Plenum.

Tolman, Deborah. (1994). Daring to desire: culture and the bodies of adolescent girls. In *Sexual Cultures and the Construction of Adolescent Identities*, edited by Janice Irvine. Philadelphia: Temple University Press.

Treboux, Dominique. and Nancy A. Busch-Rossnagel. (1991). Sexual behavior, sexual attitudes, and contraceptive use: age differences in adolescents. In *Encyclopedia of Adolescence Vol. 1 and 2.*, edited by R. Lerner, A. Petersen, J. Brooks-Gunn. New York: Garland Pub.

Ward, Janie Victoria and Jill McLean Taylor. (1994). Sexuality education for immigrant and minority students: developing a culturally appropriate curriculum. In *Sexual Cultures and the Construction of Adolescent Identities*, edited by Janice Irvine. Philadelphia: Temple University Press.

Warren, Carol. (1988). *Gender Issues in Field Research*. Beverly Hills, CA: Sage.

Winnicott, D. W. (1965). *Playing and Reality*. London: Tavistock.

Wolf, Naomi. (1991). *The Beauty Myth*. New York: William and Morrow.

Wright, David and Lori Peterson and Howard Barnes. (1990). The relation of parental employment and contextual variables with sexual permissiveness and gender role attitudes of rural early adolescents. *Journal of Early Adolescence*. 10: 382–398.

Zelnick, M., J. F. Kantner, and K. Ford. (1981). *Sex and Pregnancy in Adolescence*. Beverly Hills: Sage Publications.

Zelnick, M. and J. F. Kantner. (1980). Sexuality, contraception, and pregnancy among metropolitan area teenagers: 1971–1979. *Family Planning Perspectives*. 12: 230–237.

INDEX